MARGIT'S FIBER ART

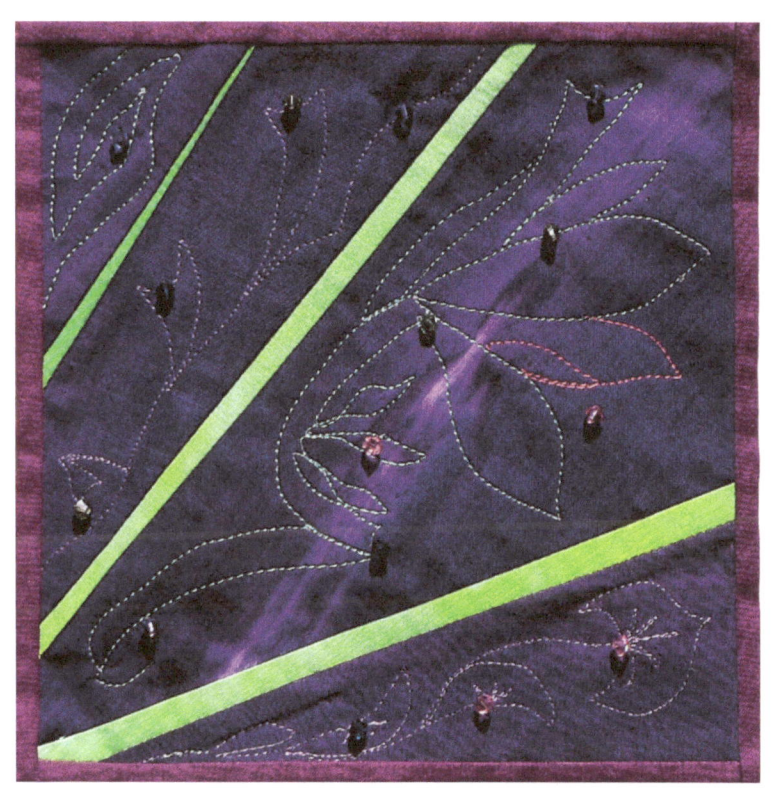

NEW DIRECTIONS

MARGIT KAGERER

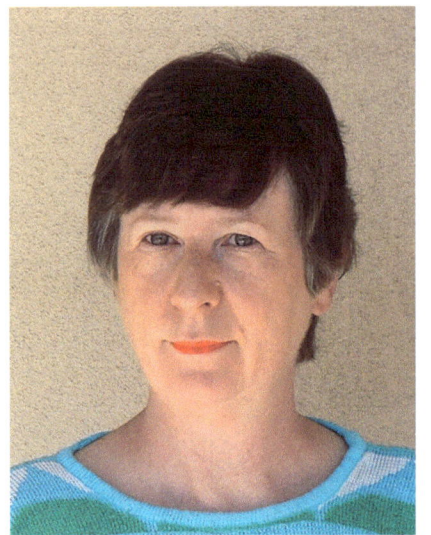

A native of Germany, fiber artist Margit Kagerer was introduced to the world of quilting and fiber art when she relocated to the United States. She had been a math teacher to 11th and 12th graders, but was unable to continue this profession. Her interest in geometry naturally led her to admire the patterns found in traditional quilts. Right from the beginning she created her own contemporary designs with geometric patterns. She was also inspired by the colors of her surrounding environment, especially the vibrant foliage in New England.

When the couple moved to Arizona, Margit was attracted by the brilliant colors and beauty of the desert. So she "painted" the dramatic Arizona scenery with fabric.

Margit's hobby of making quilts is more than just a pleasant pastime to her. It is a way of expressing herself, using her sewing skills, teaching other quilters, and as a result of all of these, winning awards for her original quilts. Inspiration can come from many sources, and she feels that working with the different fabrics gives her a creative freedom, allowing her to "transfer what I see into a picture or abstract design".
Carefree, Arizona, July 2014

For additional information please visit http://margit.artrageousfibers.net

The quilt on the front page was an experiment. I tried to sew a reversible quilt. The other side is shown on the last page.

PREFACE

When I started quilting in 1993 most of my quilts were pieced in a traditional way using commercial cotton fabrics. I taught myself many of the traditional patterns but always tried to add a contemporary twist. I was intrigued by geometric patterns and was also inspired by nature, first in New England and then in the Sonoran Desert in Arizona. I enjoyed creating my own designs immensely.

Through my membership with the Mavericks, a group of contemporary quilters and fiber artists, I was introduced to new surface design techniques and ideas. The challenges the group put together every year made me think outside the box and extended my horizon.

I also combine quilting with my hobby of photography. The images are printed on fabric and sewn together. Then the collage is enhanced with machine quilting and threadwork.

My friends and members of my quilt group know that I collect neckties. So my stash is growing and I am planning on more quilts with ties.

In my first book I showed 90 quilts that I had created until 2009.
The following small images recapture 6 of them.

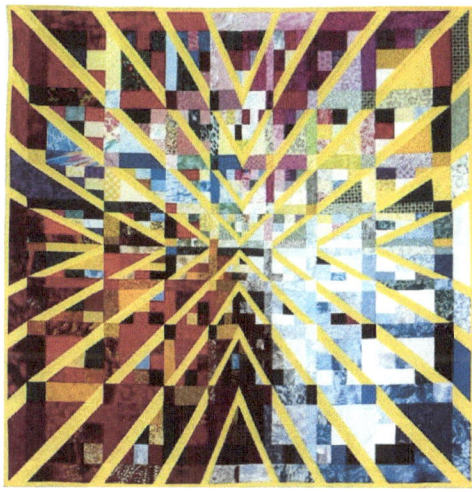
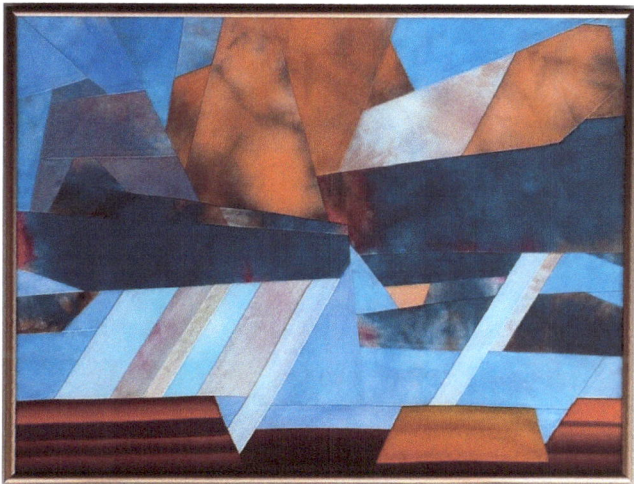

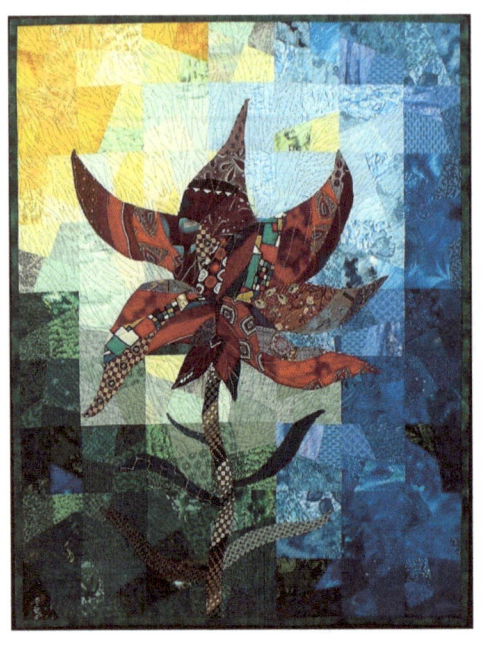

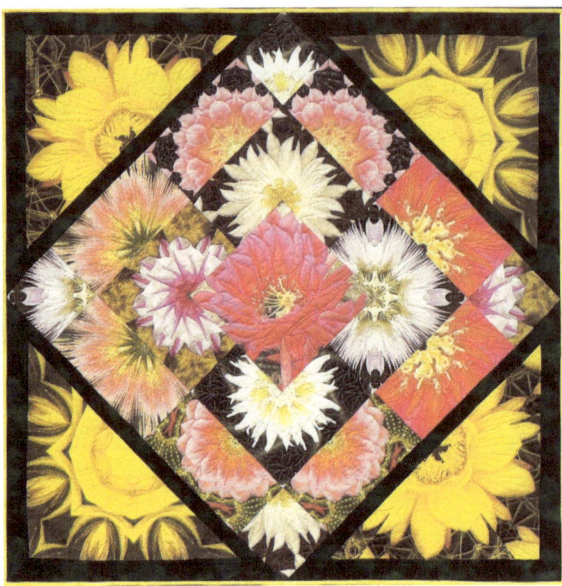

The sequel MARGIT'S FIBERART – NEW DIRECTIONS contains most of the pieces I made during the last 5 years. By learning new techniques and using a variety of materials I changed my style and I am heading into new directions.

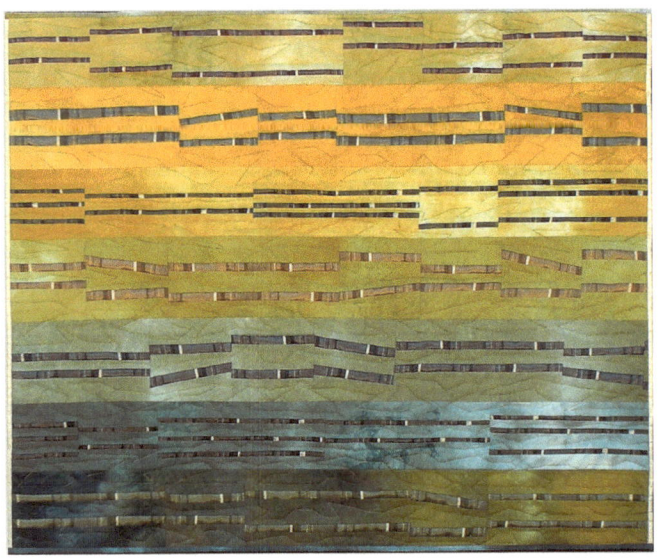

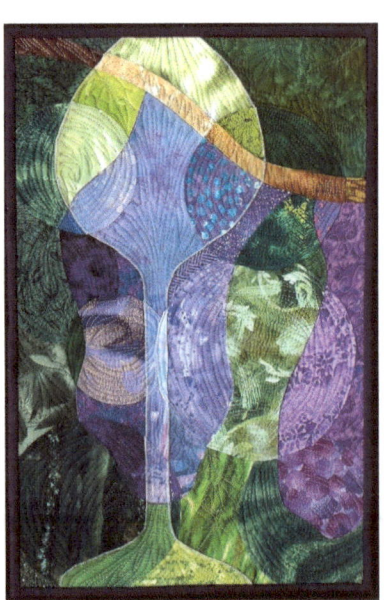

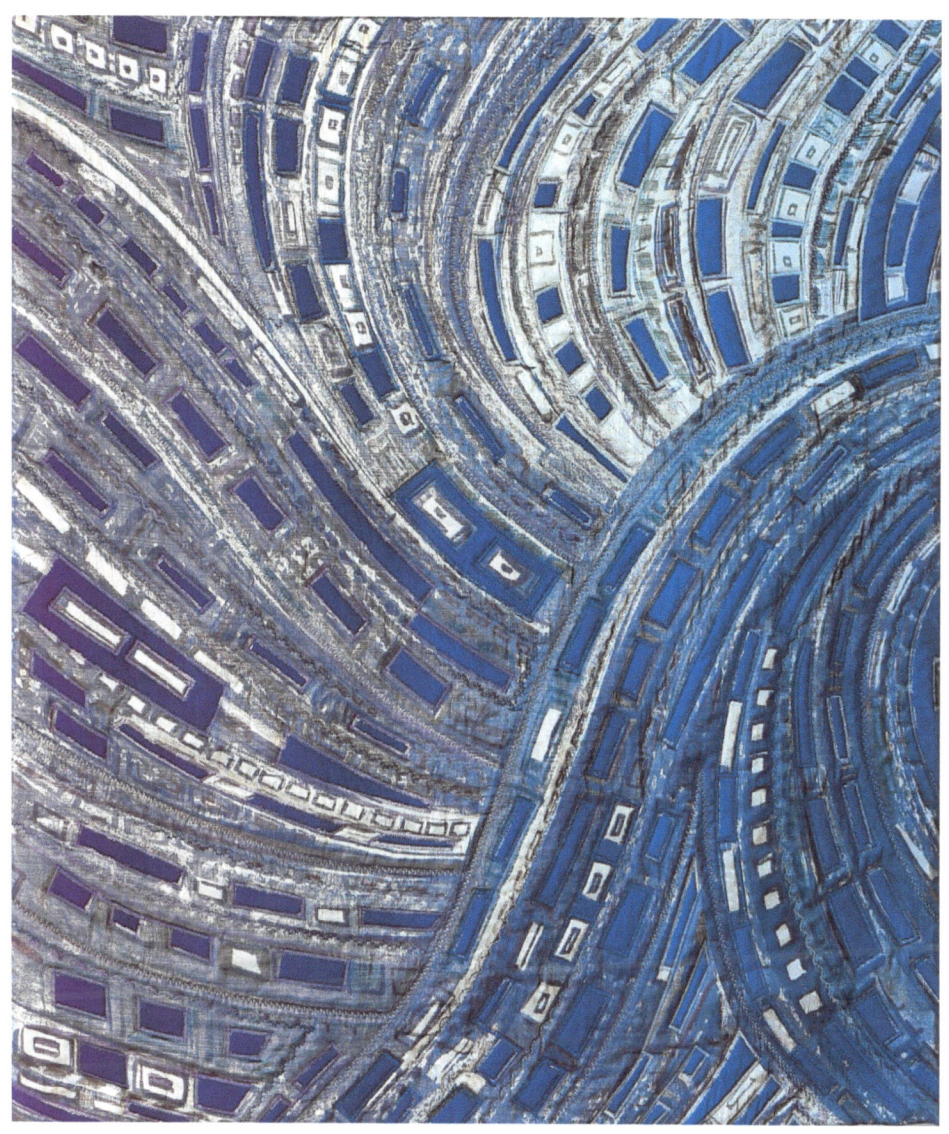

SHAPES OVER BLUE AND PURPLE

© Margit Kagerer, 2008, 25" x 29""

A few years ago I started a series called 'Shapes' with panels of decorator fabric, which could not be used for traditional piecing. So I came up with the idea to put the sheer fabric over a background fabric, stitch the design through all the quilt layers, and cut away the top fabric in selected areas. I experimented with different colors for the background fabric

My most recent quilt 'Shapes over Blue and Purple' was selected to be featured in the book '500 Art Quilts', published by Lark Books.

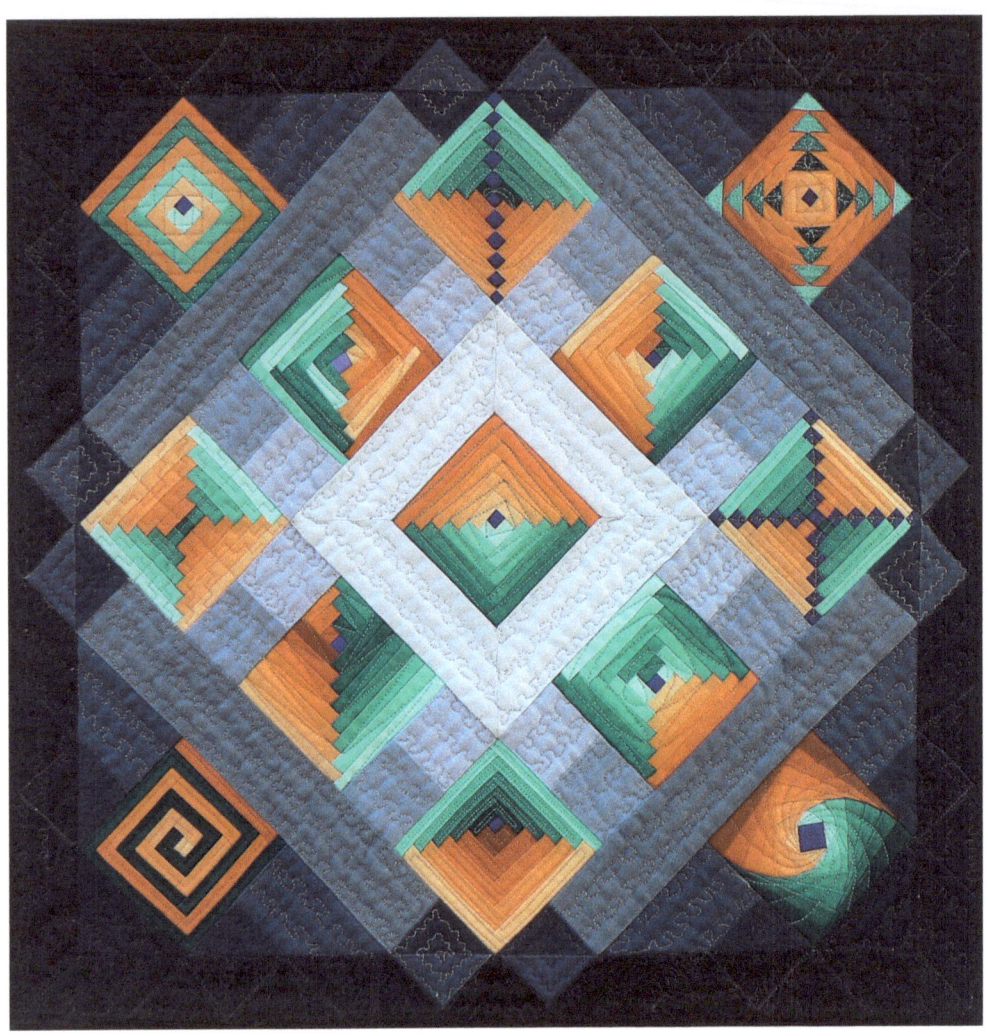

ONE PLUS TWELVE

© Margit Kagerer, 2010, 18" x 18"

The log cabin block is my favorite. Even as a contemporary quilter, I like to explore the different variations of this traditional block. All the 13 blocks were quilted with a different pattern.

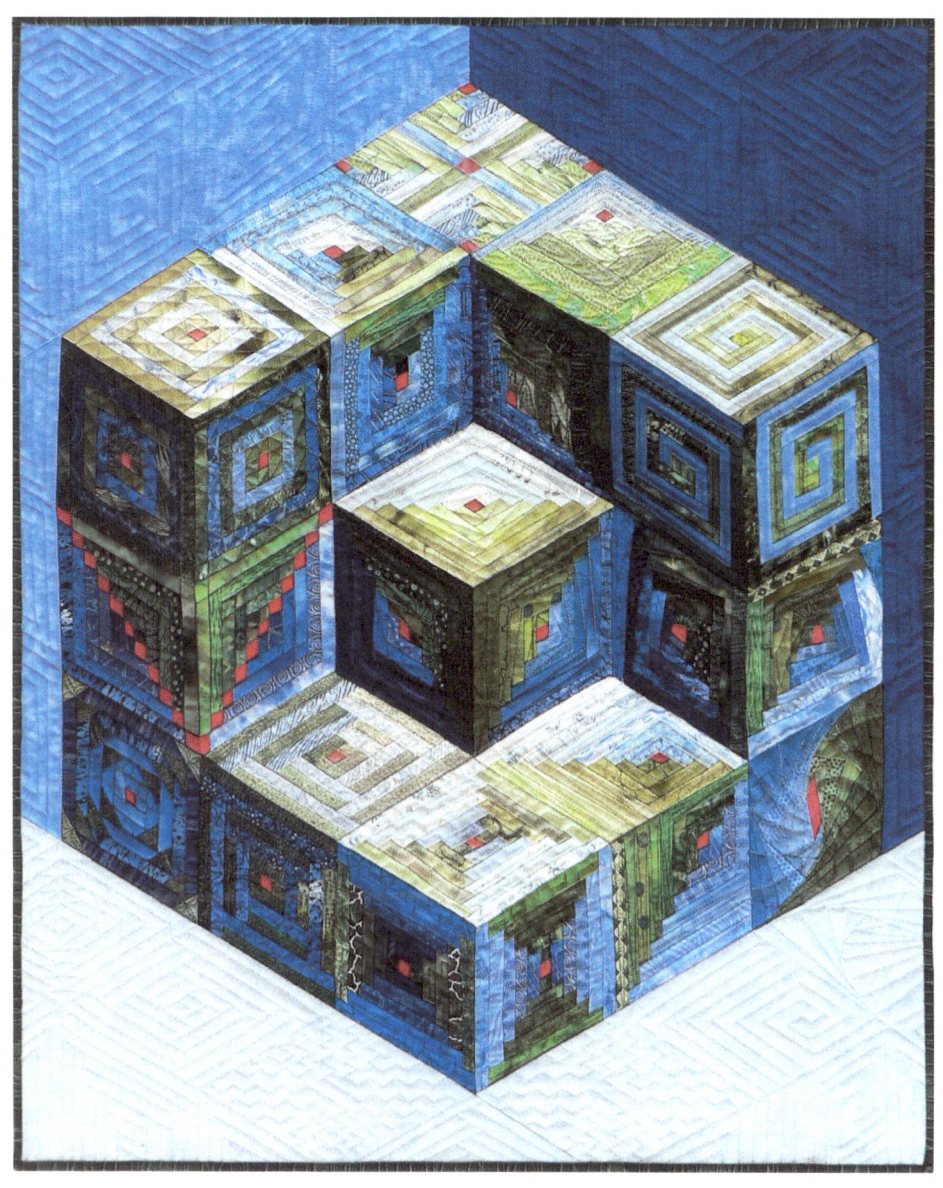

LOG CABIN CUBICLES

© Margit Kagerer, 2011, 18" x 21"

The quilt contains the traditional log cabin block and 12 variations. I put them on the sides of tumbling blocks and created a 3-D look.

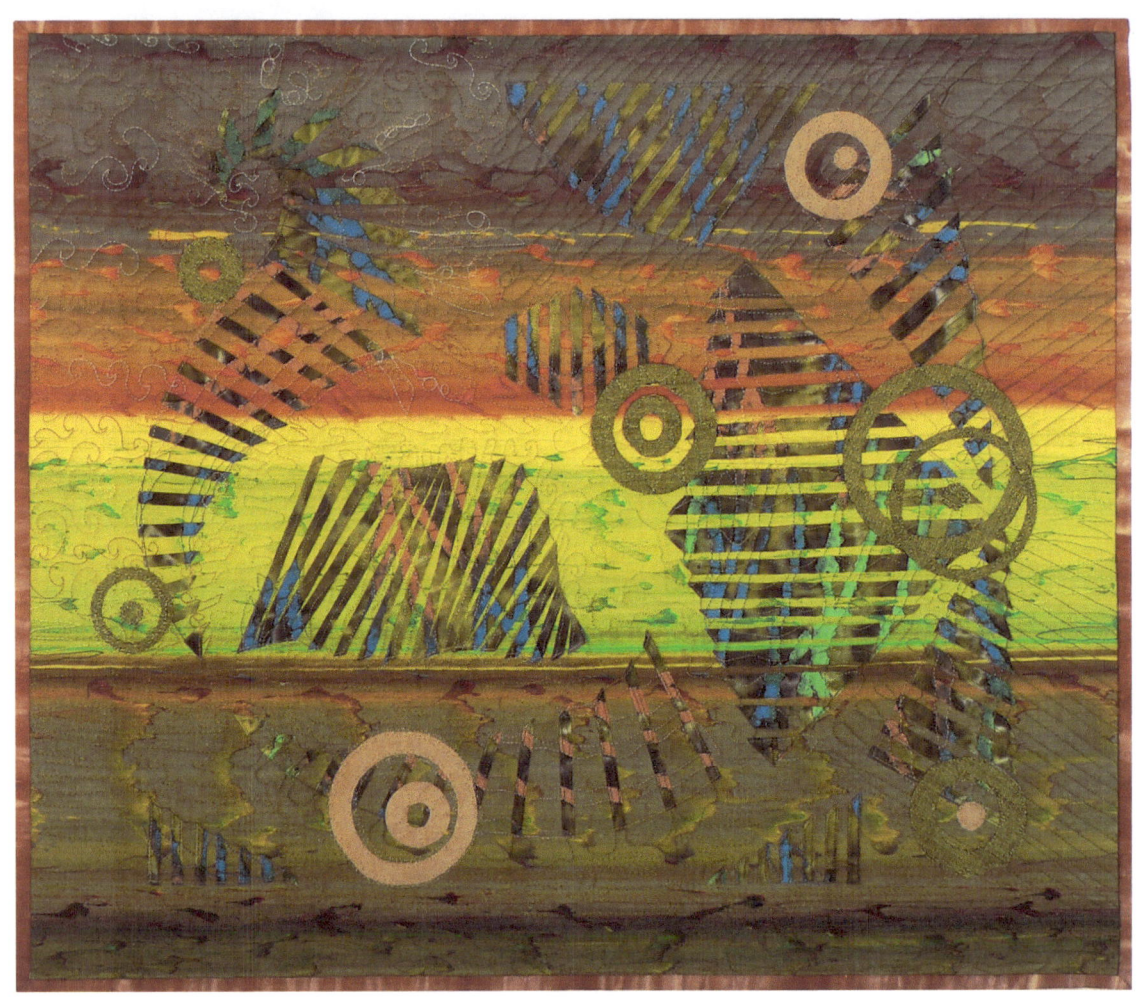

FANTASY

© Margit Kagerer, 2013, 24" x 20"

I took a workshop with Chris Lynn Kirsch on Parallelisms. It was a fun class using '... parallel strips, geometric spirals, and imagination...'

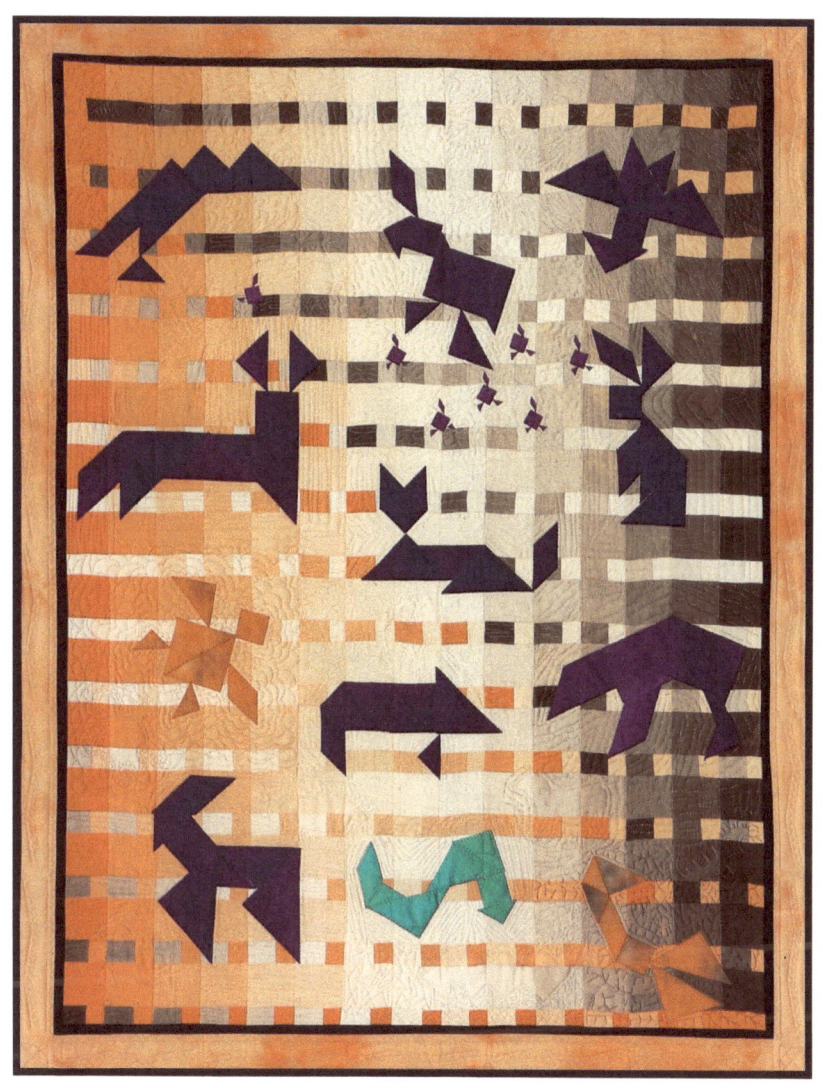

TANGRAMS AND PETROGLYPHS

© Margit Kagerer, 2012, 37" x 49"

Years ago I started a quilt with hand dyed fabrics. I liked the gradations of the orange and brown fabrics but not the overall look of the piece. So I decided to appliqué some geometric shapes. On my search for interesting shapes I found tangrams on the internet. The tangram is a dissection puzzle consisting of seven flat shapes, called *tans*, which are put together to form shapes. The objective of the puzzle is to form a specific shape (given only an outline or silhouette) using all seven pieces, which may not overlap. I chose animals of the desert and quilted corresponding petroglyphs.

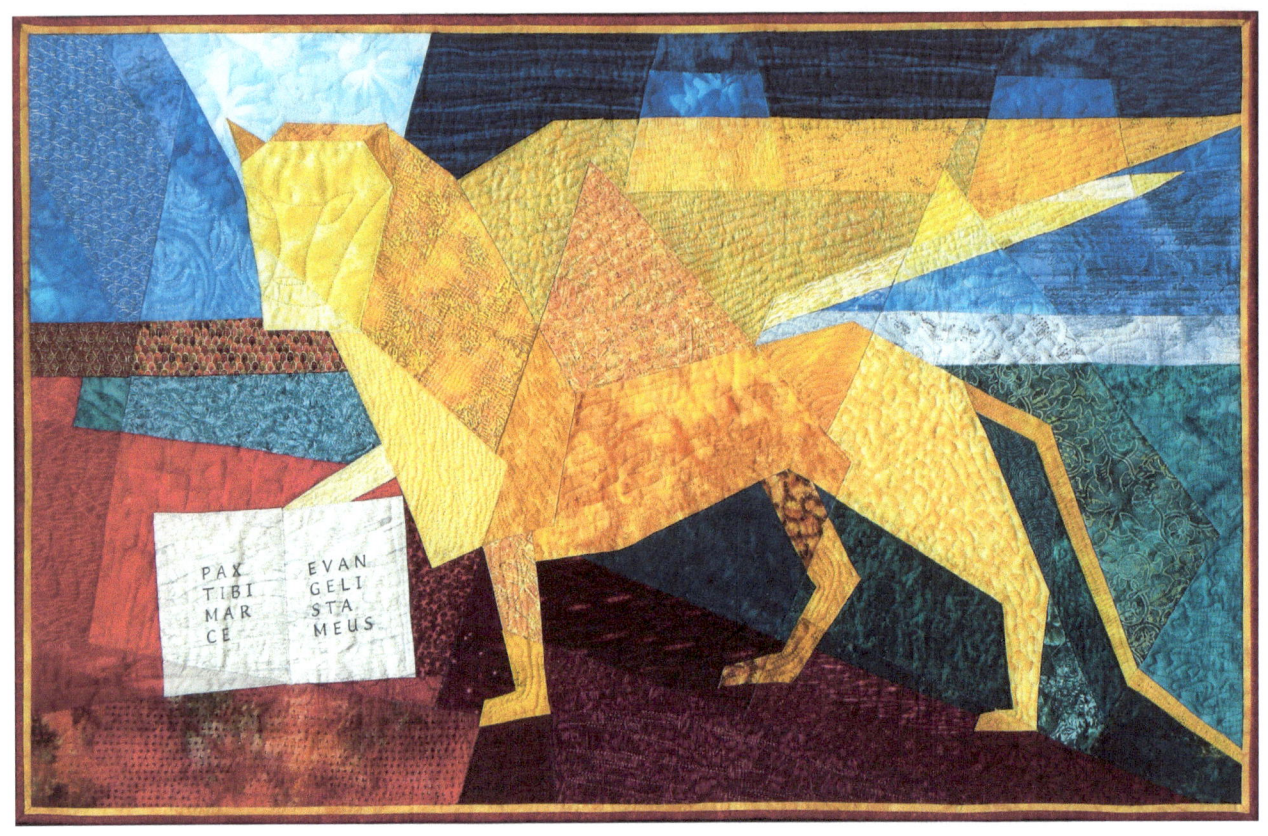

DER LOEWE VON ST. MARKUS

(THE LION OF SAINT MARK)

© Margit Kagerer, 2010, 41" x 25"

The quilt was a commission for the German 'Honorable Ambassador to the Republic of Venice'. I transformed an old painting by Carpaccio 'Il Leone di Venezia' into a modern design with the background colors 'lagoon green', 'Venice red', and 'Byzantine night blue'. By defining areas with lighter values I indicated shapes of sails because Venice was a major maritime power during the Middle Ages and Renaissance. Since parts of the opera 'Tristan und Isolde' were composed in Venice, I machine quilted a few lines of the famous duet from act II.

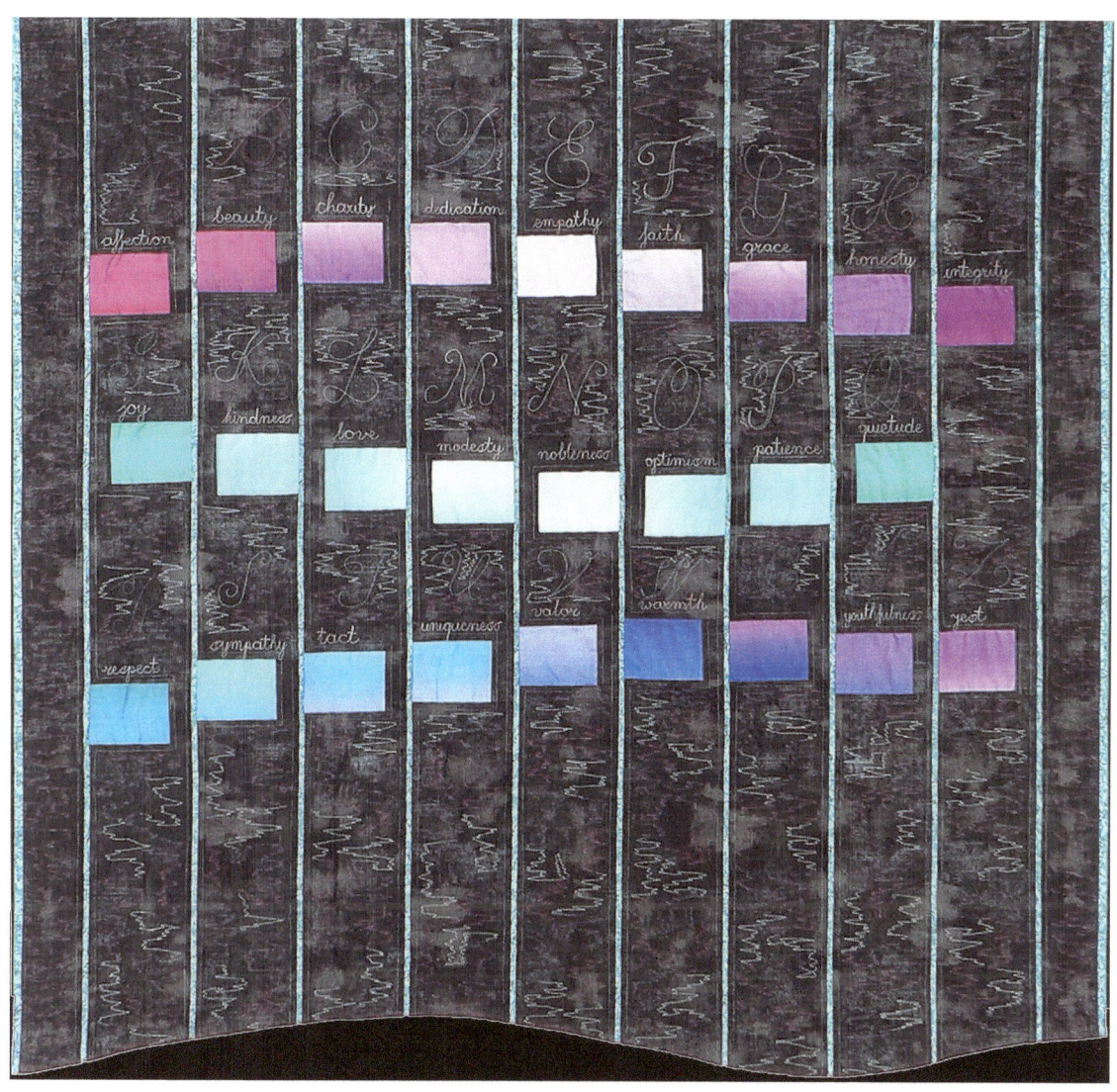

THE ALPHABET OF VIRTUES

© Margit Kagerer, 2011, 46" x 44"

Virtues and values guide life in every culture. I have chosen 25 different virtues, each beginning with a letter from our alphabet, as the theme for this quilt. (Since I could not find an appropriate word starting with an X I have left this area open.) The colored rectangles underneath each word remain undefined to encourage each viewer to express their personal interpretation.

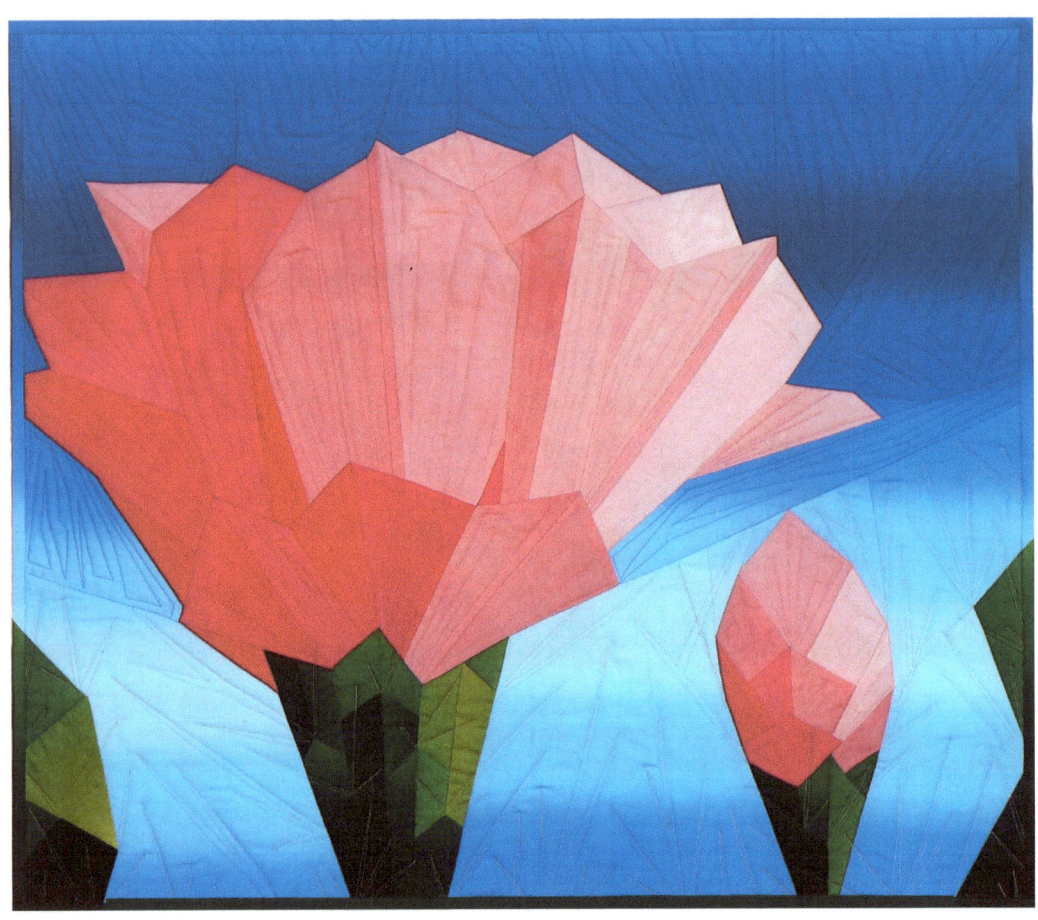

CACTUS BLOSSOMS

© Margit Kagerer, 2011, 31" x 26"

Spring is the most colorful season in the desert when wildflowers and cacti are in full bloom. Some of the cacti are inconspicuous during the year but their flowers burst into such intense colors that they can be seen from far away. This inspired me to make a quilt with brilliant fabrics. To emphasize the harsh environment of the desert, I used straight seam and quilting lines for the blossoms and the spines.

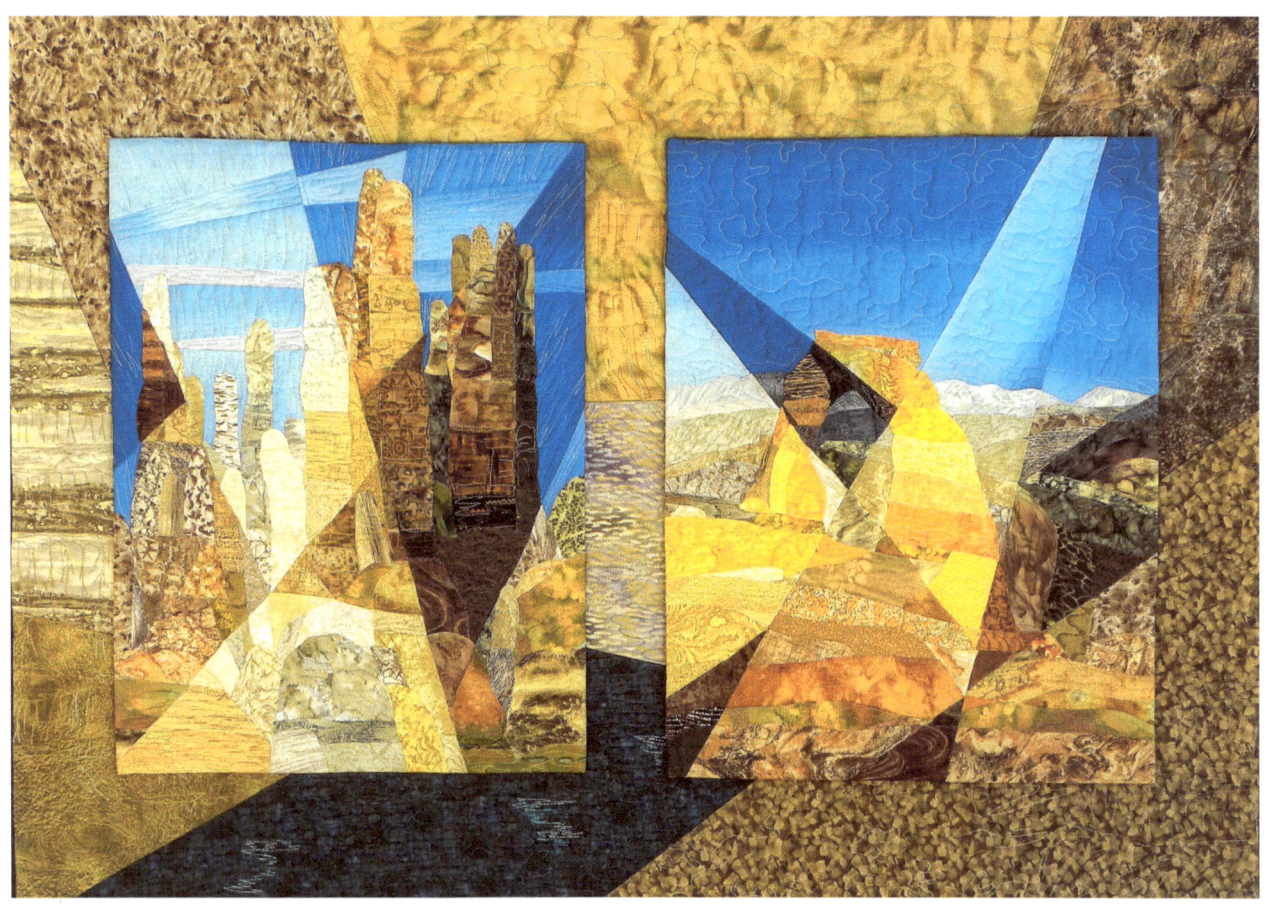

DESERT SOLITAIRE

© Margit Kagerer, 2012, 48" x 33"

In 1975 while visiting the Southwest of the US as a tourist from Germany, I bought Abbey's book as a souvenir and to learn more about the desert. With my basic knowledge of the English language, it was hard for me to understand the full meaning of the book. Years later after my husband and I had moved to Arizona I read the book again. Now I understand Abbey's passion for the Southwest and I share his love of the desert.

For my quilt I chose three locations from the book: Arches National Park, the Maze in Canyonlands, and the Grand Canyon for the back panel.

The quilt was made for an exhibition '**Fiber, Facts, and Fiction**' that the Mavericks organized.

The following 4 door quilts were made for the Mavericks exhibition '**Thresholds**'

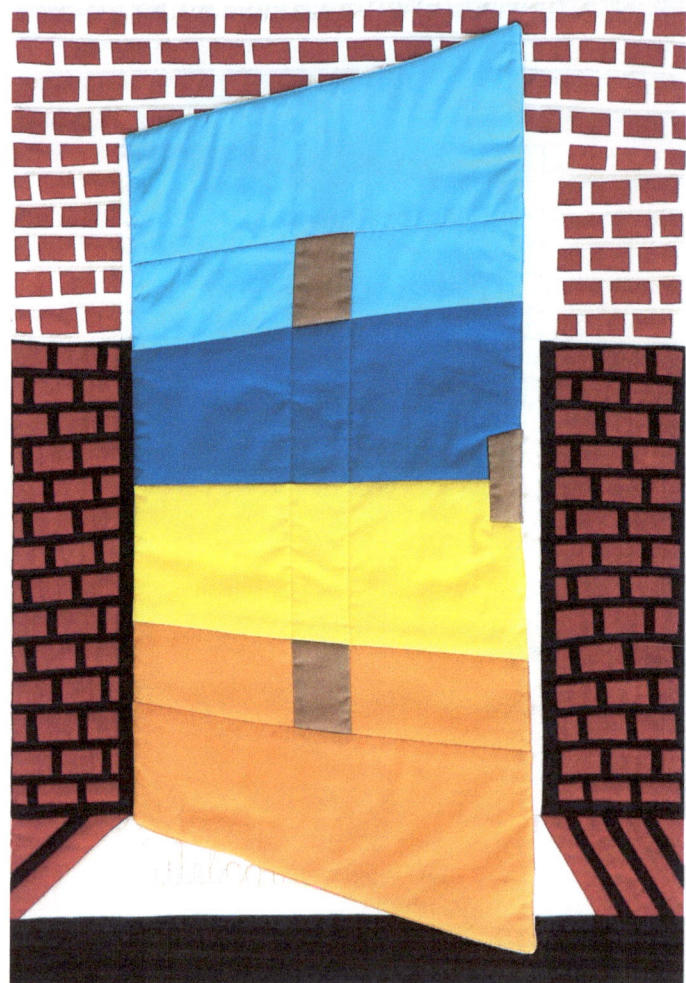

ALBERS' DOOR

© Margit Kagerer, 2013, 18" x 24"

Josef Albers (1888 –1976) was a German-born American artist and educator whose work formed the basis of some of the most influential and far-reaching art education programs of the twentieth century. Part of my design for this door is from his book 'Interaction of Color'.

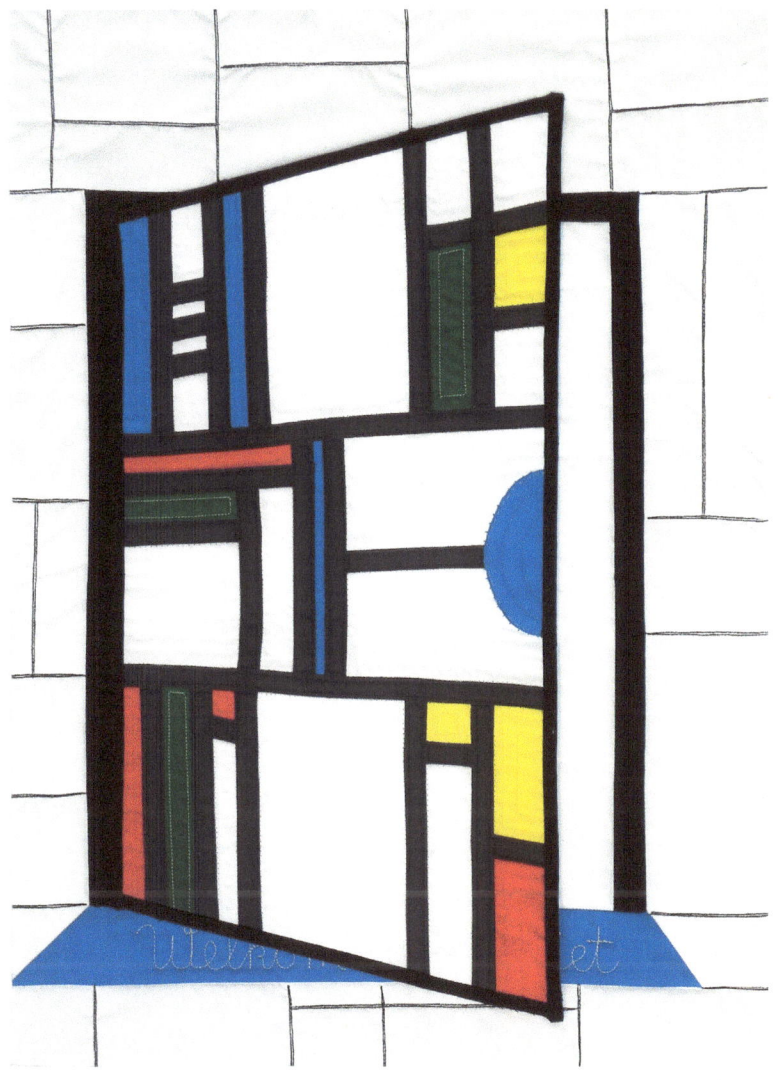

MONDRIAN'S DOOR

© Margit Kagerer, 2013, 18" x 24"

Pieter Cornelis "Piet" Mondrian (1872 –1944) was a Dutch painter. He was an important contributor to the De Stijl art movement. He evolved a non-representational form which he termed neoplasticism. This consisted of white ground, upon which was painted a grid of vertical and horizontal black lines and the three primary colors.

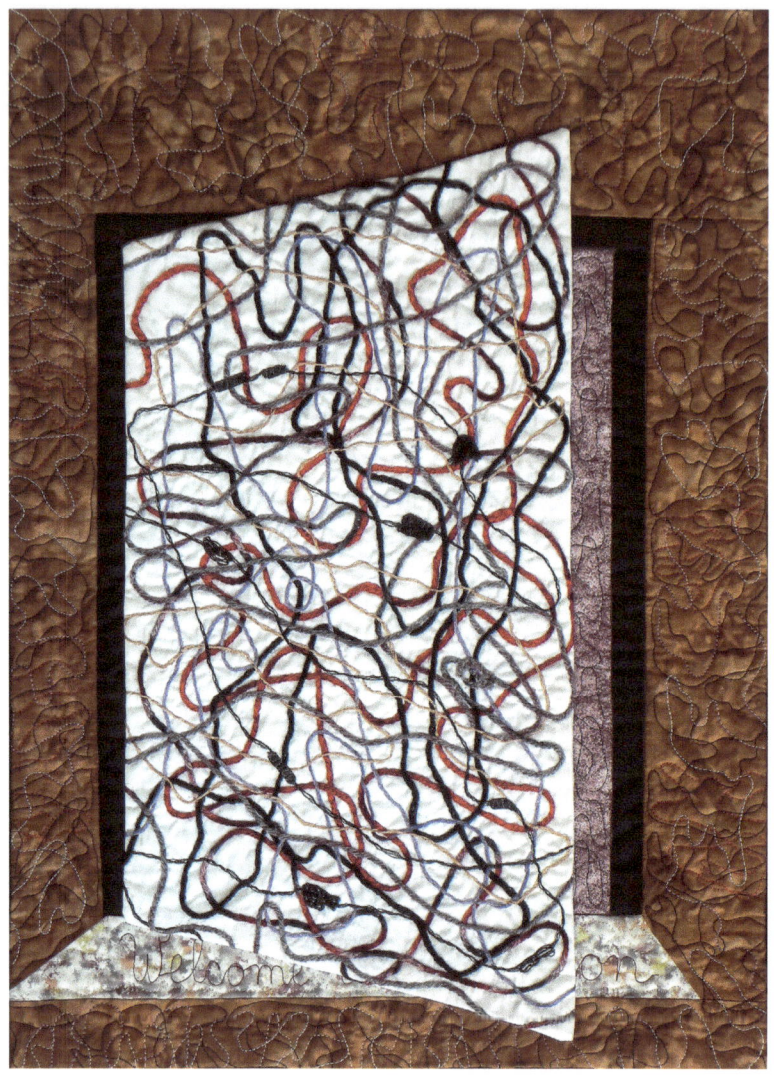

POLLOCK'S DOOR

© Margit Kagerer, 2013. 18" x 24"

Paul Jackson Pollock (1912 –1956) was an influential American painter and a major figure in the abstract expressionist movement. He was well known for his unique style of drip painting. I imitated his technique by using threads instead of paint for the flowing lines. I had a lot of fun with my thread doodling.

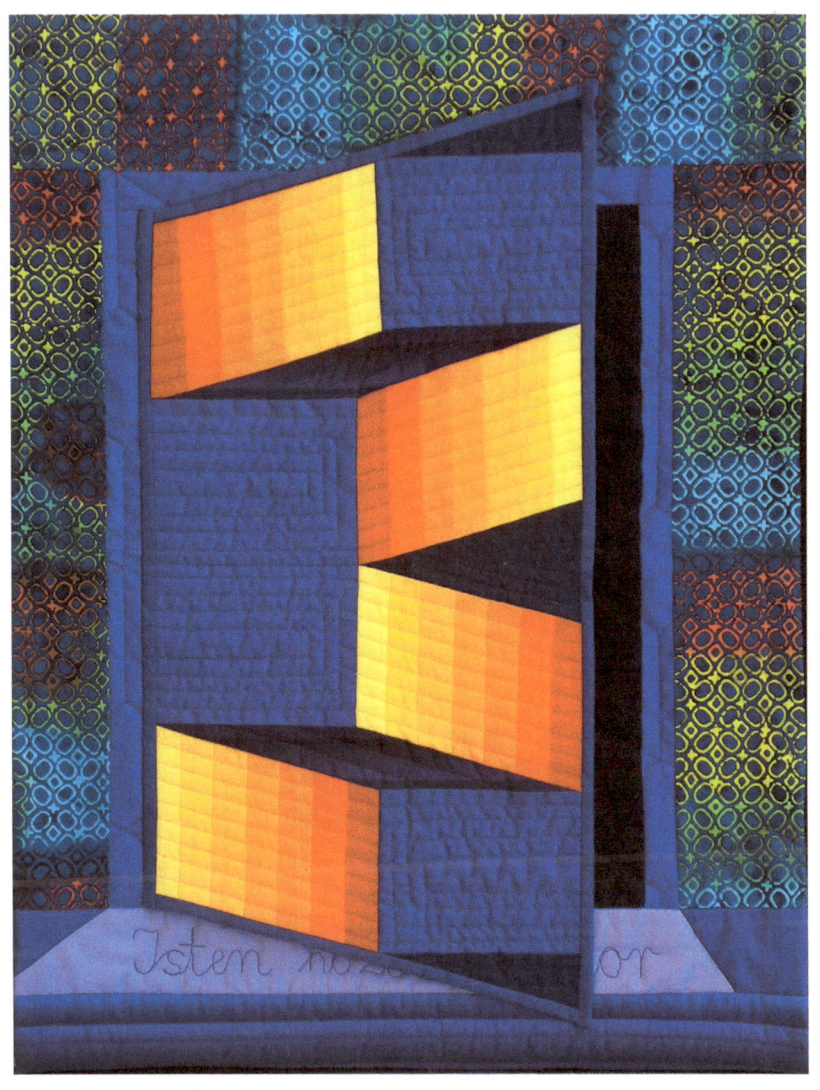

VASARELY'S DOOR

© Margit Kagerer, 2013, 18" x 24"

Victor Vasarely (1906 –1997) was a Hungarian-French artist and is widely accepted as a "grandfather" and leader of the op art movement. I like his bold colors, the geometric shapes, and the optical illusion in his work.

The following 2 quilts were the results of a challenge by the Mavericks to use more than 50% black fabric in a 24" x 24" quilt.

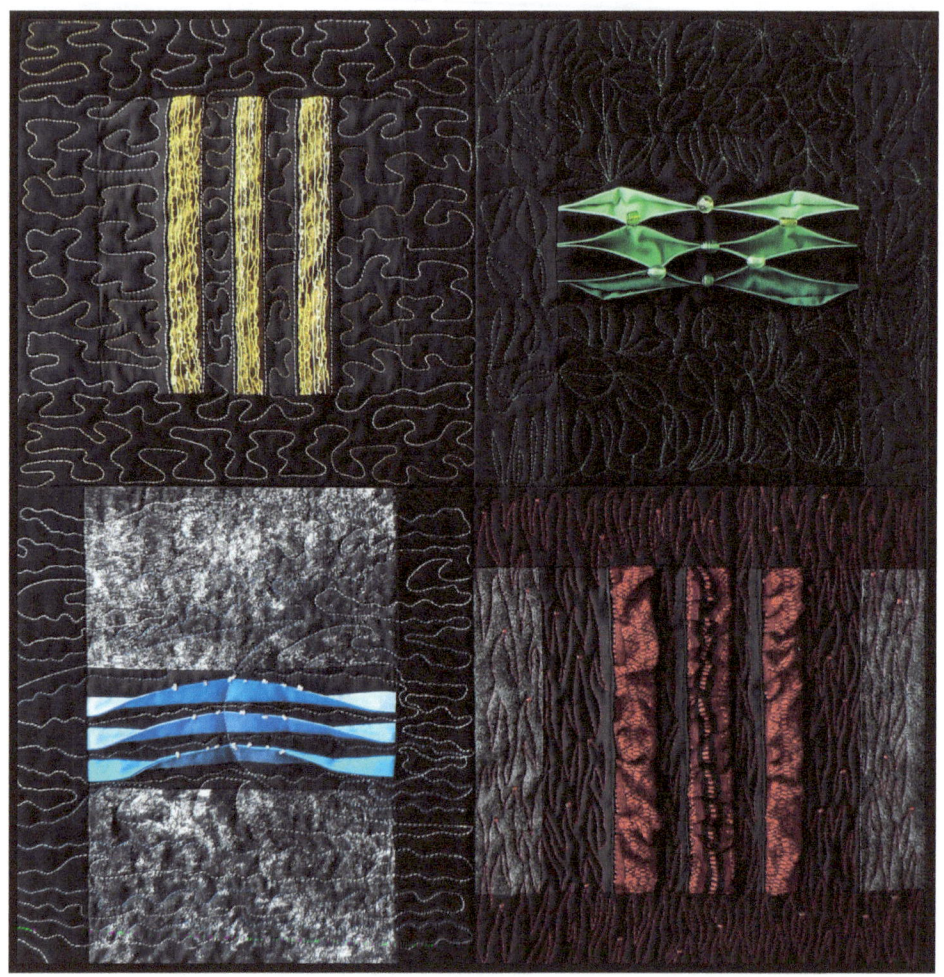

FOUR ELEMENTS

© Margit Kagerer, 2009, 24" x 24"

I tried some surface design techniques like pleads.

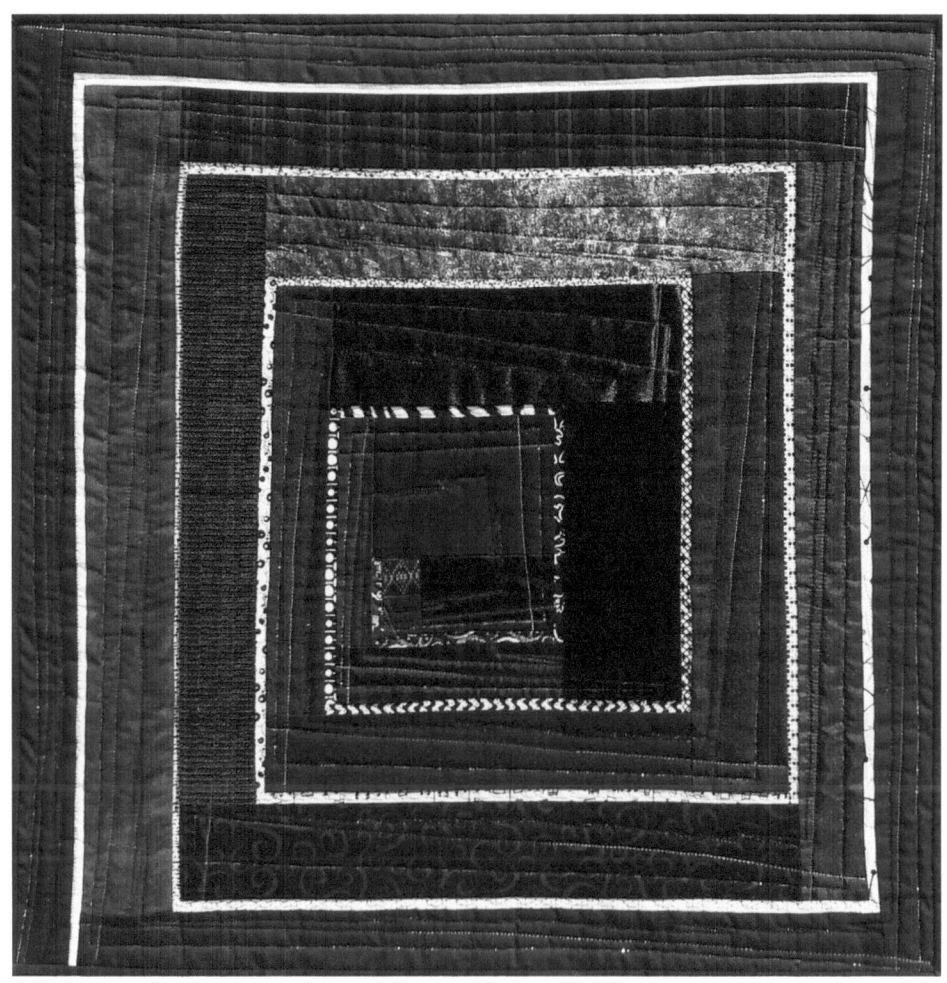

VARIATIONS OF BLACK

© Margit Kagerer, 2009, 24" x 24"

19 black fabric pieces with different textures like cotton, velvet, silk, polyester, corduroy were sewn into this log cabin style quilt.

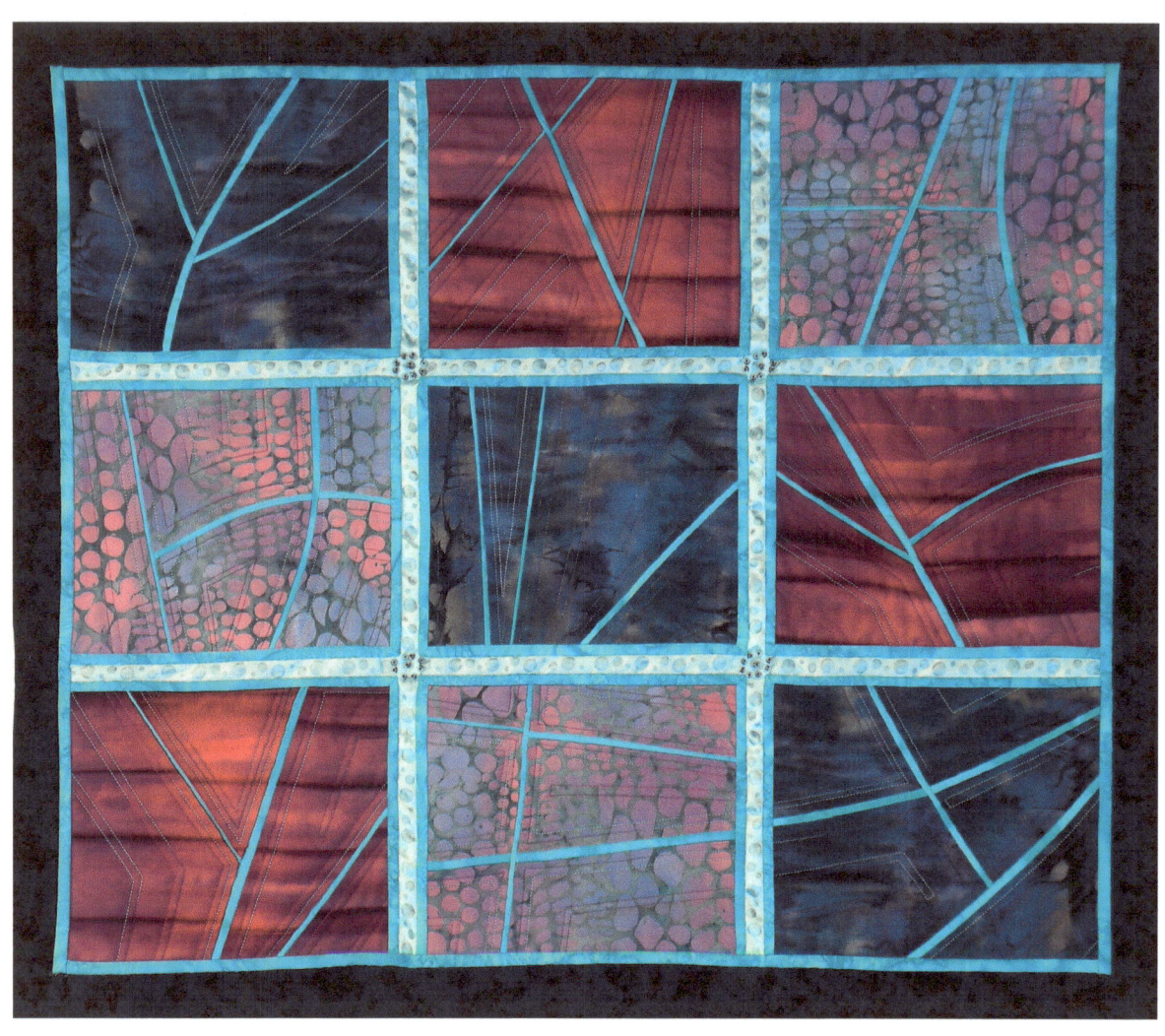

NINE-PATCH CHALLENGE

© Margit Kagerer, 2012, 29" x 25"

This was a good practice piece for sewing very skinny insets.

NIGHT

© Margit Kagerer, 2013, 17" x 52"

This quilt is a first for me in many regards. Instead of working with bright colors I picked a dark color palette. I did not piece the quilt top but quilted just one single panel. And I enjoyed improvising the free motion quilting lines.

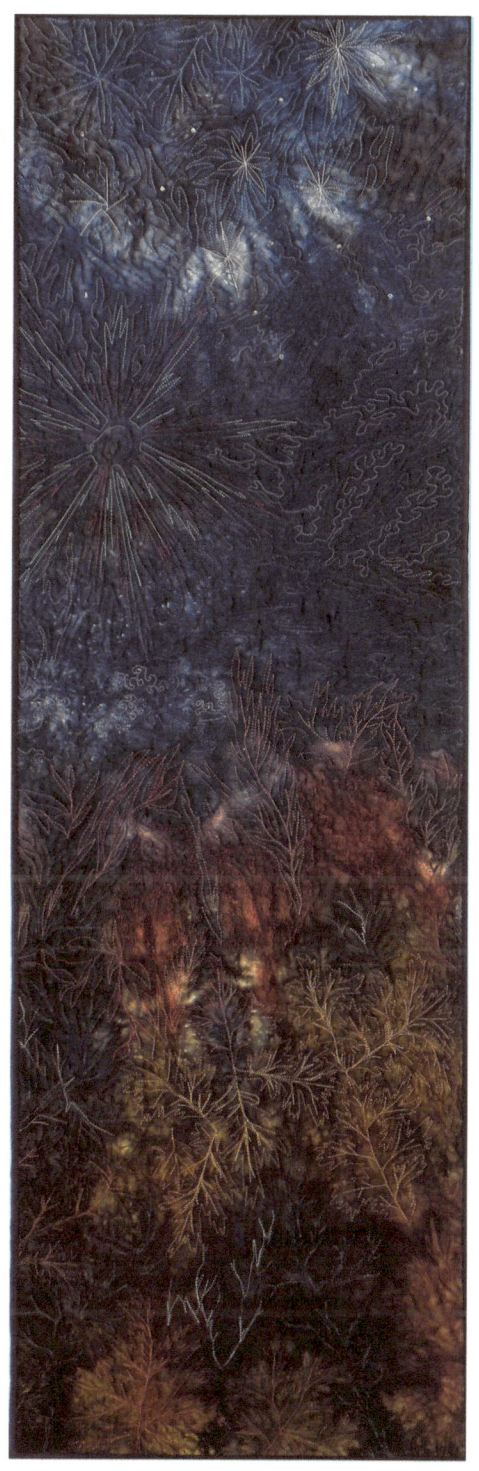

USING PRINTS ON FABRIC

    I like to use images in my quilts. The photos were either printed on our own oversized plotter or by a service that specializes in print on fabric. In some cases I first manipulated the photos on the computer for an abstract design. The quilting lines or the threadwork always add another design element to the piece.

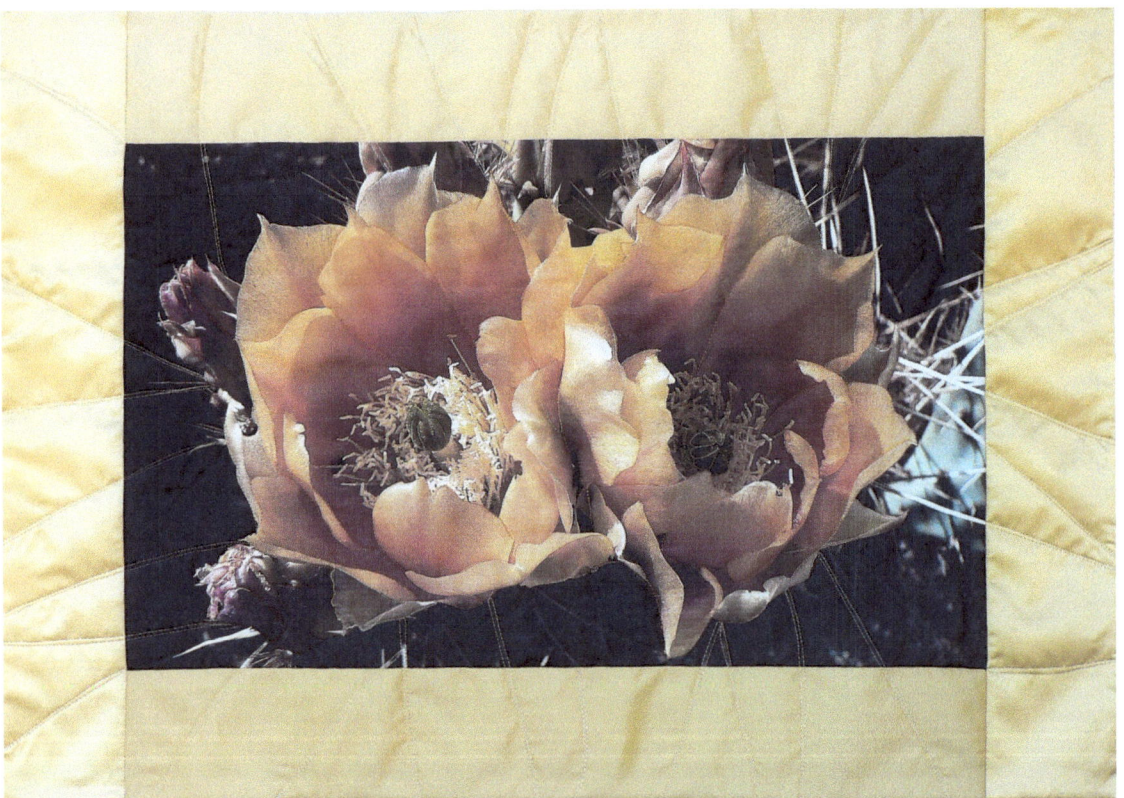

PRICKLY PEAR FLOWERS

© Margit Kagerer, 2009, 32" x 22"

The print of a prickly pear flower looks really good on silk.

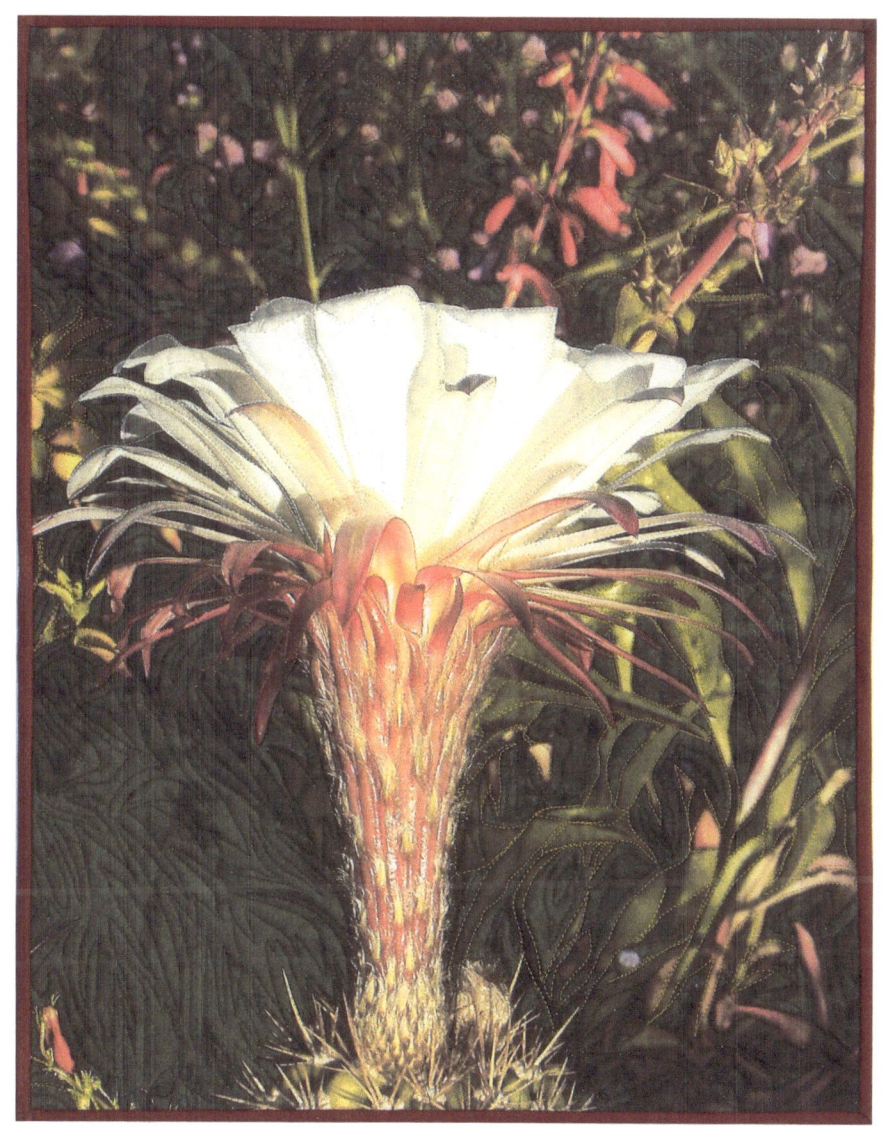

BEAUTY AT NIGHT

© Margit Kagerer, 2010, 16" x 20"

Those beautiful cereus flowers bloom only one night.

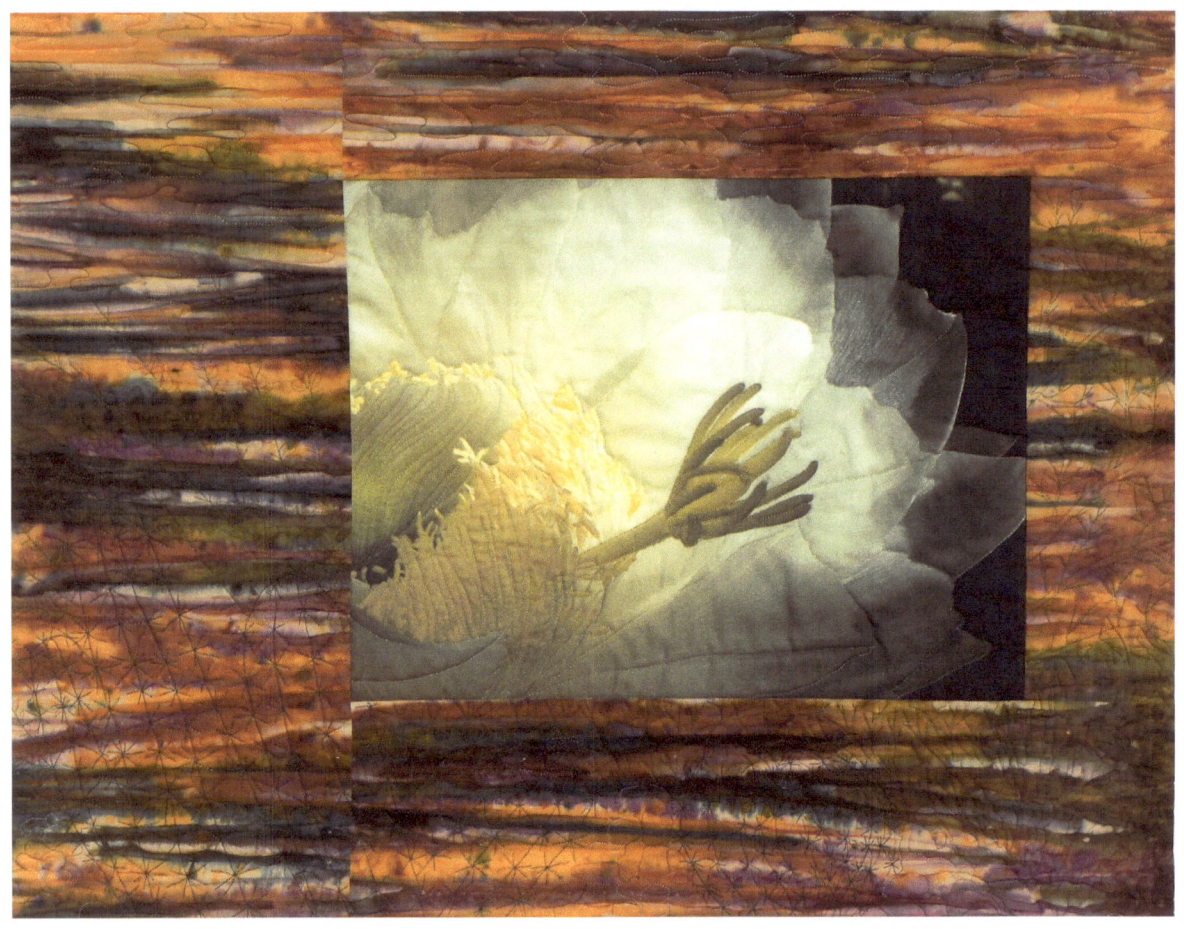

CONTRAST

© Margit Kagerer, 2013, 36" x 27"

Conditions in the desert are harsh: low rainfall, high temperatures, poor soil. Trees and shrubs adapted by eliminating leaves - replacing them with thorns. The spines of the cacti protect them from animals, shade them from sun, and collect moisture. Yet in this rough environment cacti produce the most beautiful, delicate flowers.

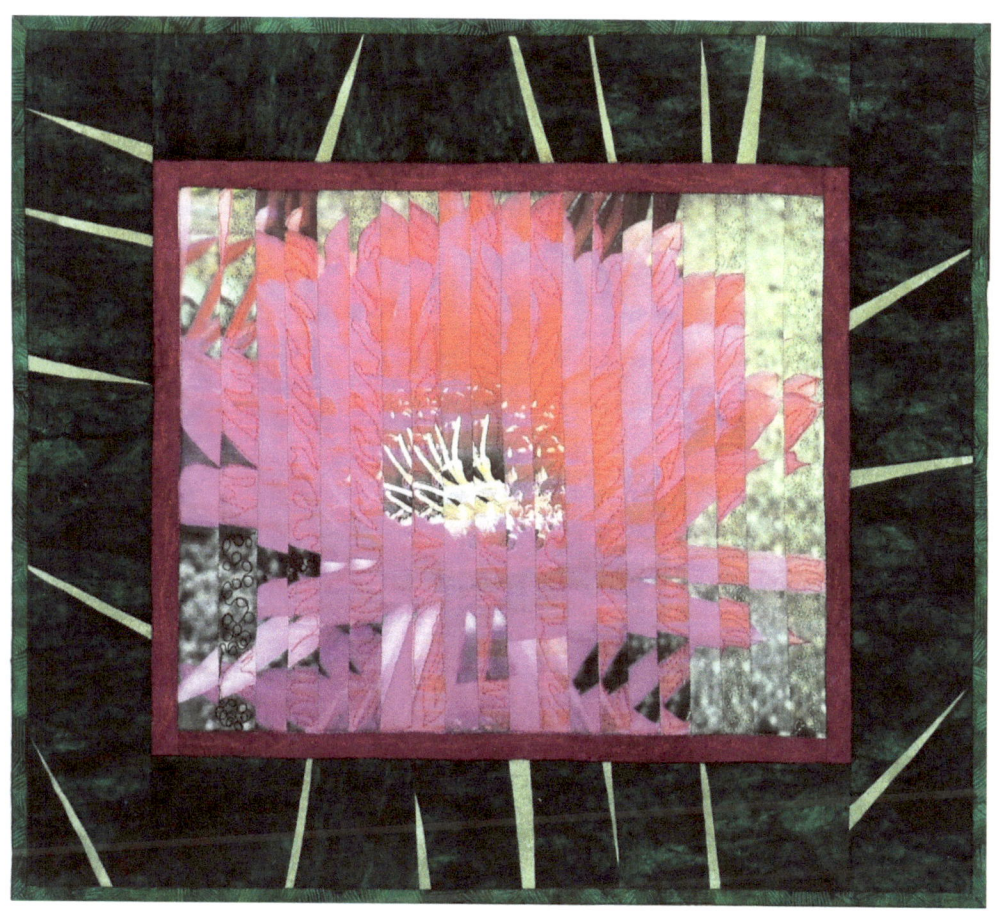

CEREUS, CEREUS

© Margit Kagerer, 2011, 17″ x 15″

I experimented with 2 identical prints that were cut in stripes and then sewn together again. This gives an interesting blurry effect.

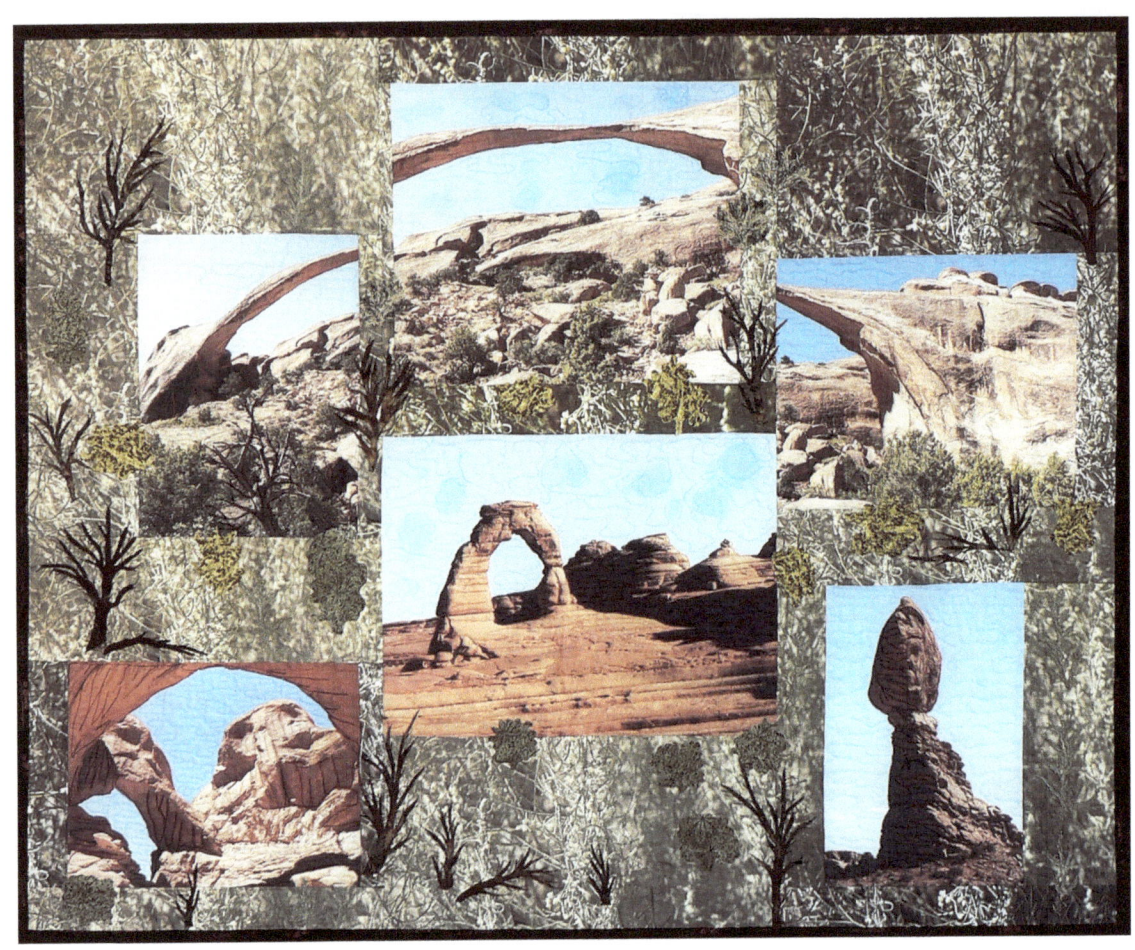

DELICATE EROSIONS

© Margit Kagerer, 2010, 44" x 34"

I love Arches National Park in Utah. On our last visit I took many photos with a quilt in mind. It was hard to choose the right photos. Landscape Arch is considered the longest natural arch in the world with a span of 290 feet. I also picked double-arch and balanced rock. My very favorite arch, Delicate Arch, became the focal point.

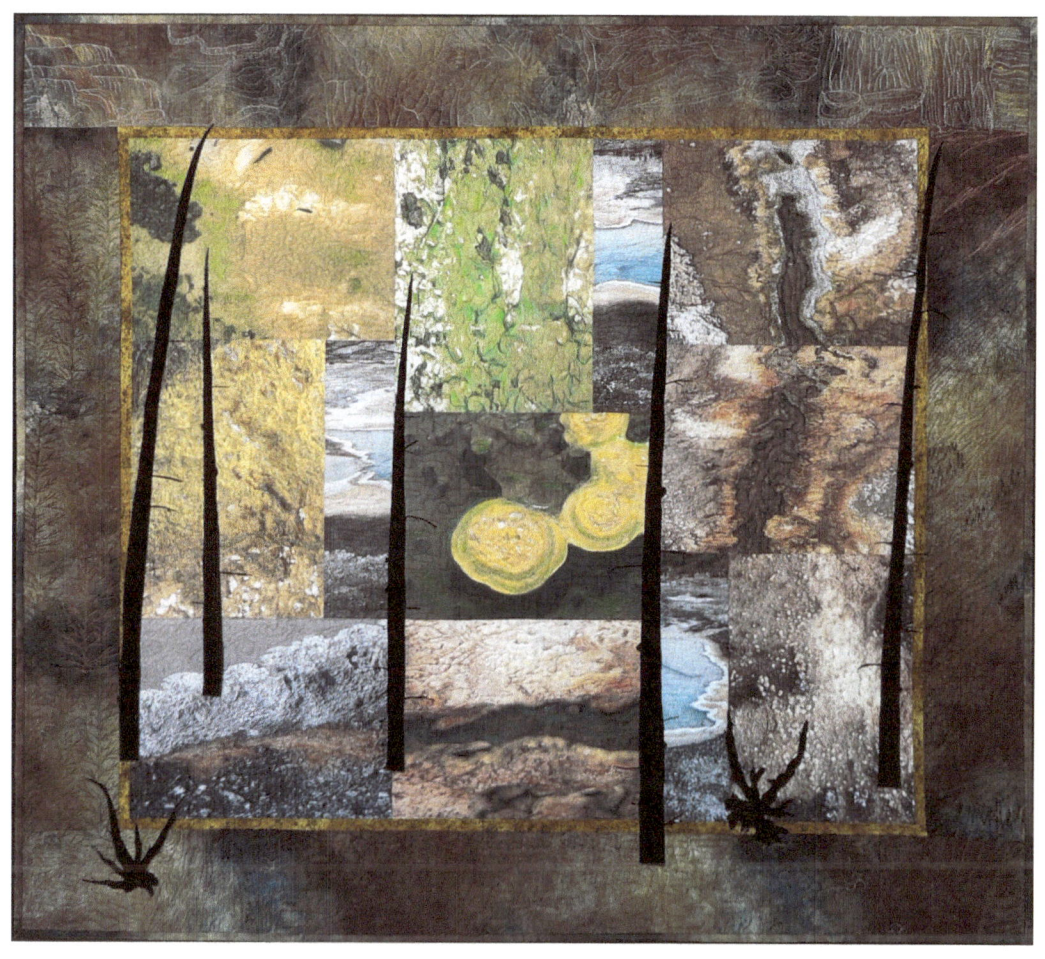

THERMAL LANDSCAPE

© Margit Kagerer, 2014, 43" x 38"

On our most recent visit to Yellowstone National Park I took many close-up photos of the pools, mud pots, and rock formations. The details look like miniature landscapes. The large forest fires of 1988 burnt nearly one third of the park. Amazingly black tree trunks still stand upright and are taller than the newly grown trees. They form a stark contrast to the colorful surface.

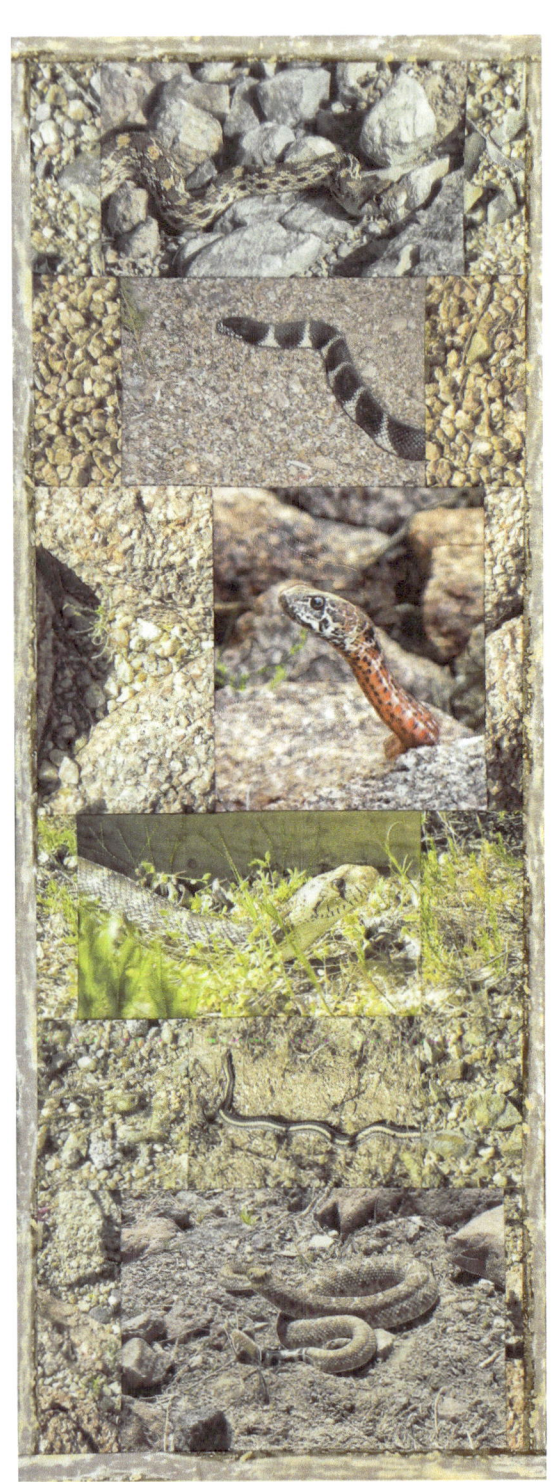

HIDDEN BEAUTIES

© Margit Kagerer, 2014, 18" x 48"

As a child I was afraid of even touching the photo of a snake. Who would have ever thought that one day I make a quilt with my own snake photos? Well. My husband took the photo of the rattlesnake.

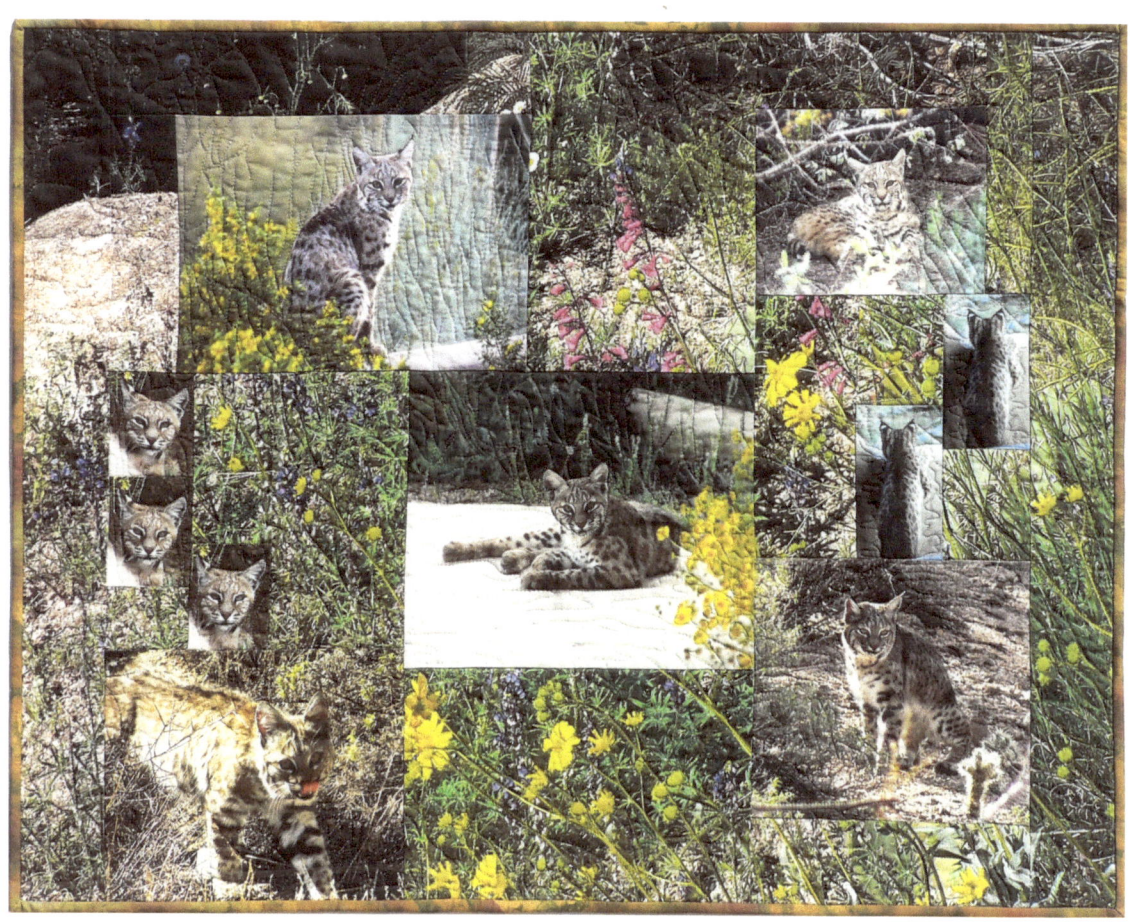

BOBCATS IN MY BACKYARD

© Margit Kagerer, 2010, 30" x 23"

I am always excited when a bobcat visits our backyard. Sometimes a mother bobcat leaves her kitten with us while she hunts for food. The kittens sleep or play until she comes back. I have many photos for more quilts.

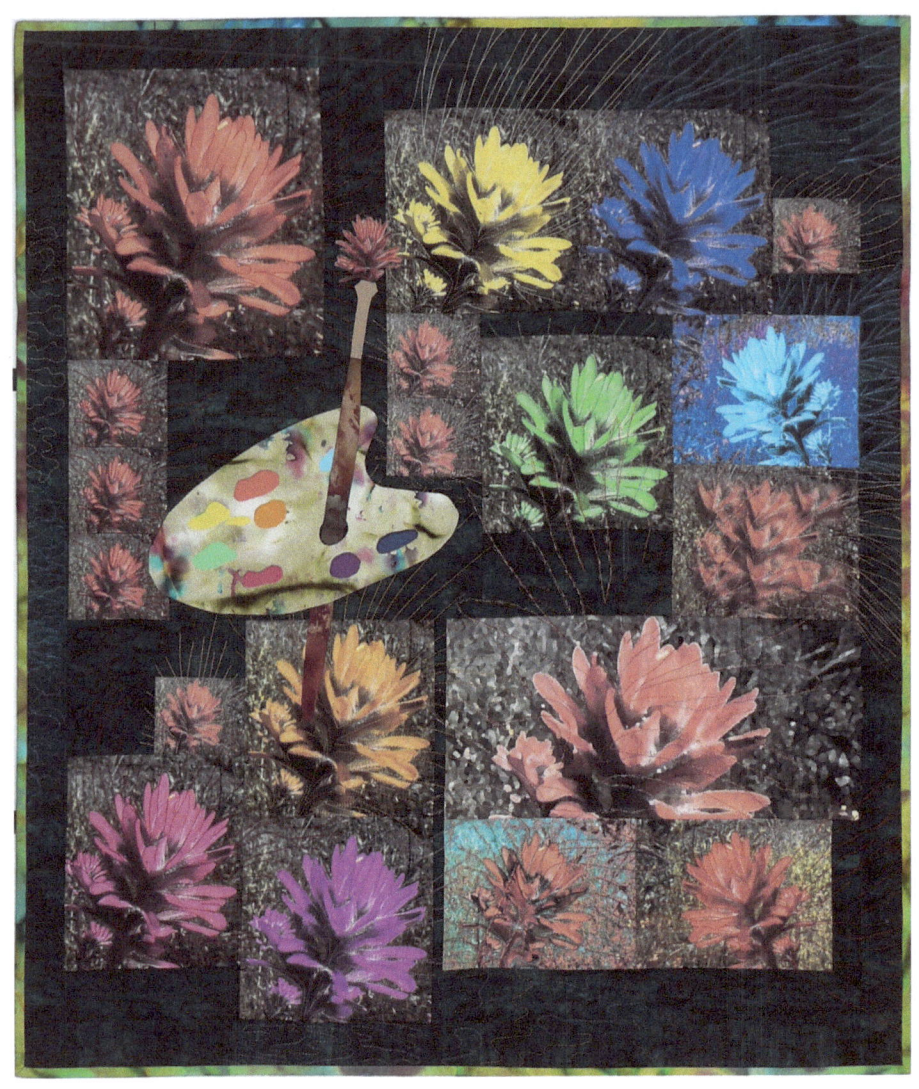

INDIAN PAINTBRUSH

© Margit Kagerer, 2010, 31" x 34"

The Paintbrush evoked the Native American legend of a young brave who tried to paint the sunset with his war-paints. Frustrated that he could not match the brilliance of nature, he asked for guidance from the Great Spirit. The Great Spirit gave him paintbrushes laden with the colors he so desired. With these, he painted his masterpiece and left the spent brushes in fields across the landscape. These brushes sprouted the flowers, which inspired me for this quilt. I thought it might be fun to 'dip' the leaves in different paints and create an artist's palette.

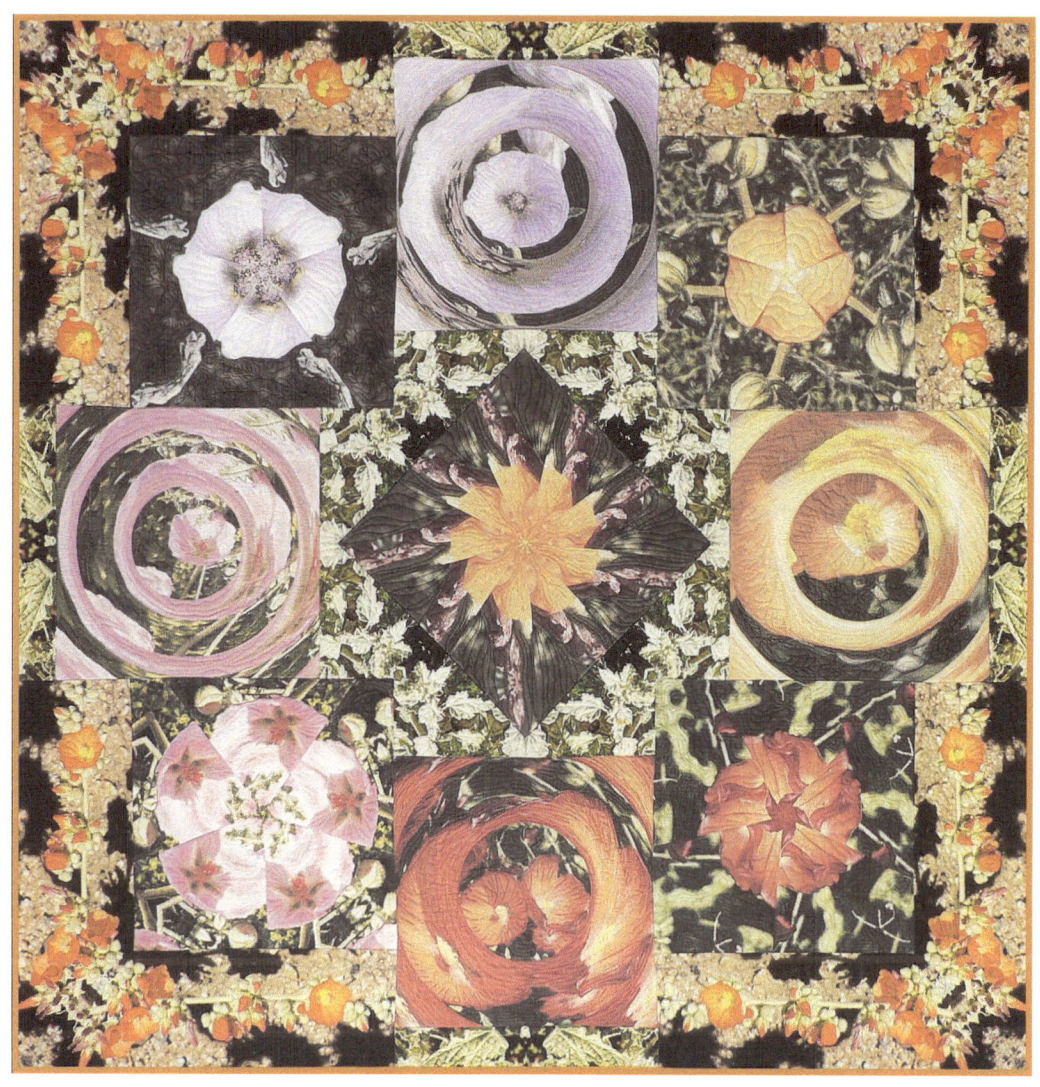

GLOBEMALLOW KALEIDOSCOPE

© Margit Kagerer, 2009, 44" x 44"

Globemallows come in many colors: most of them are orange, some are red, pink, or lavender. I love taking photos of those wildflowers. I modified the images on the computer, printed them on fabric, and composed a kaleidoscope-like setting.

In 2012 the quilt was chosen for the exhibition Lov'N Arizona at Phoenix Sky Harbor International Airport. It is now in the permanent collection of the Phoenix Airport Museum.

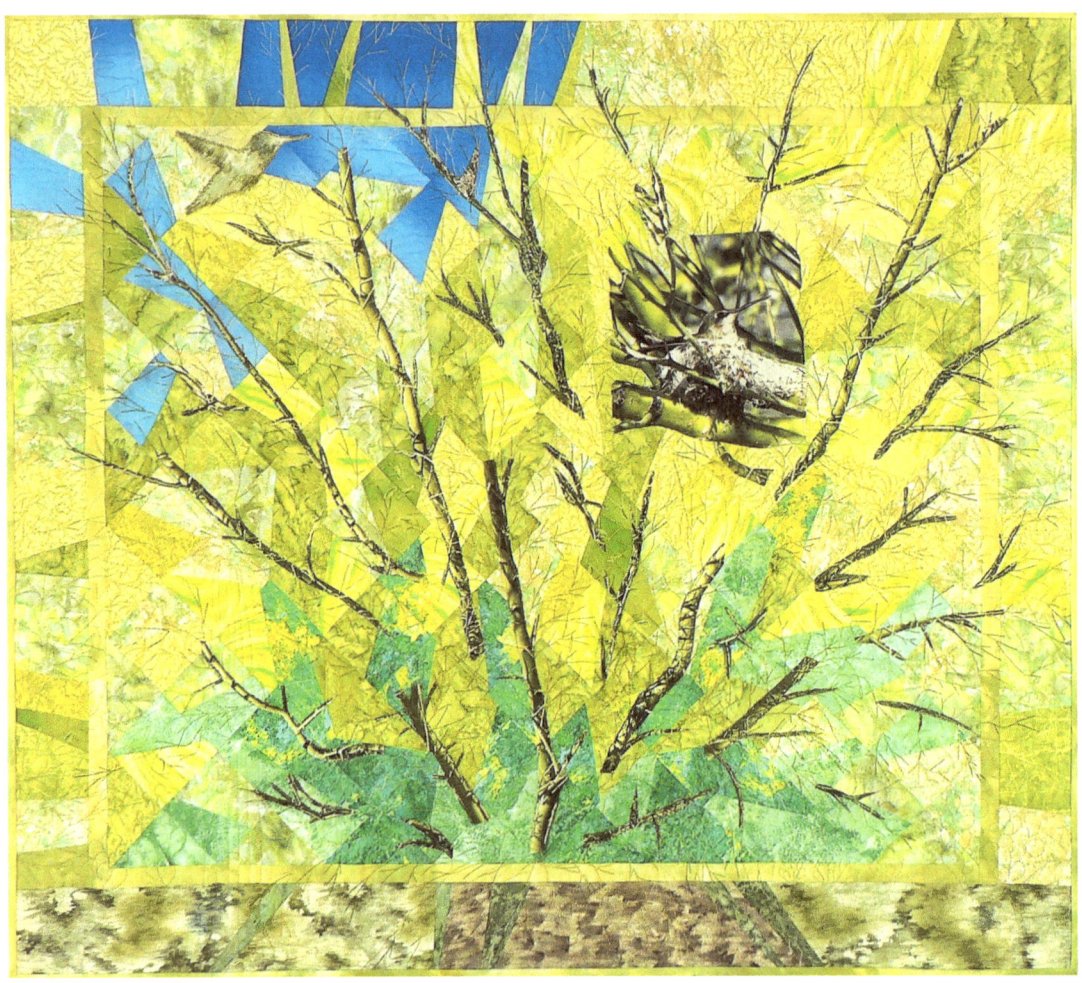

SONORAN SPRING

© Margit Kagerer, 2012, 40" x 35"

I am looking at the thicket of green branches and twigs of a paloverde tree and I see thousands of delicate yellow blossoms. At the peak of spring in the Sonoran Desert the paloverdes decorate the desert with a splendid yellow blanket. The intensity of the yellow takes my breath away.

A female hummingbird has built a little nest on a branch and she is expecting two tiny baby birds.

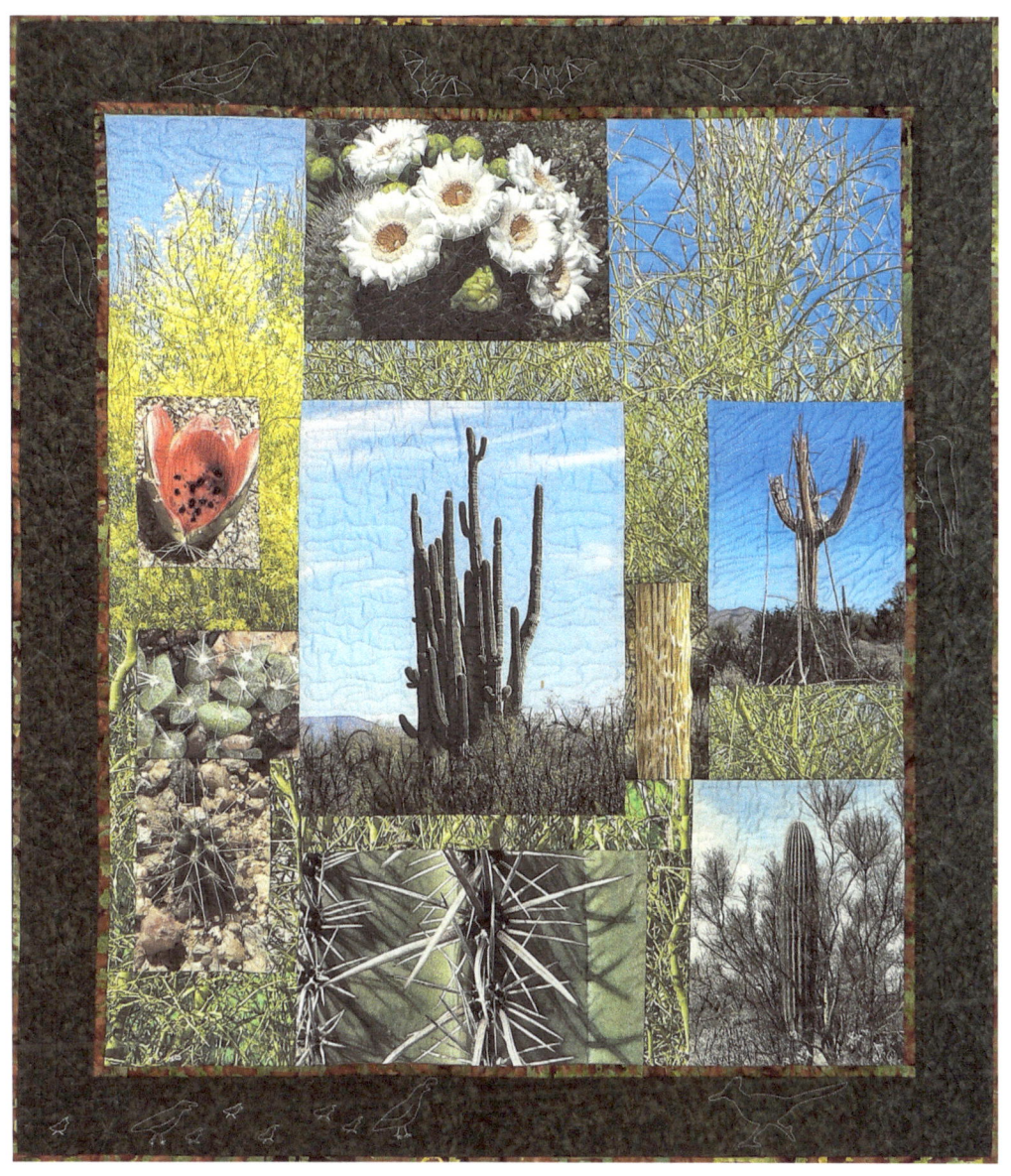

LIFE CYCLE OF THE SAGUARO

© Margit Kagerer, 2011, 41" x 46"

I love all the different regions of Arizona but the Sonoran Desert is my favorite part. My photography and my art quilts are inspired by the diverse flora and fauna. Nothing symbolizes the desert better than the Saguaro, my favorite cactus.

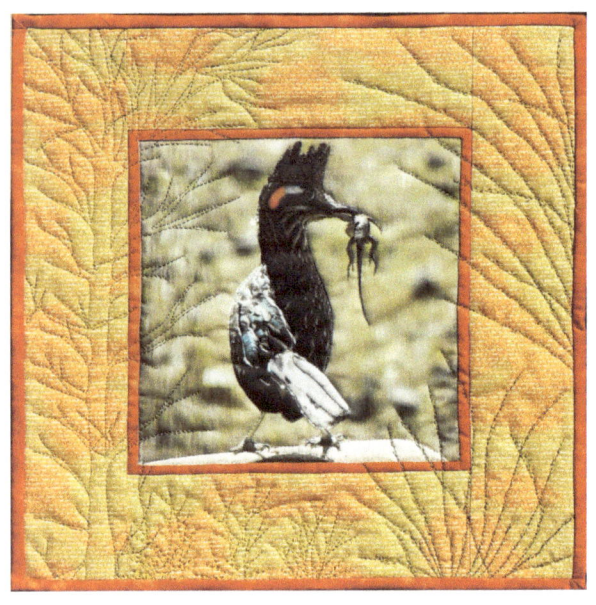

COURTSHIP

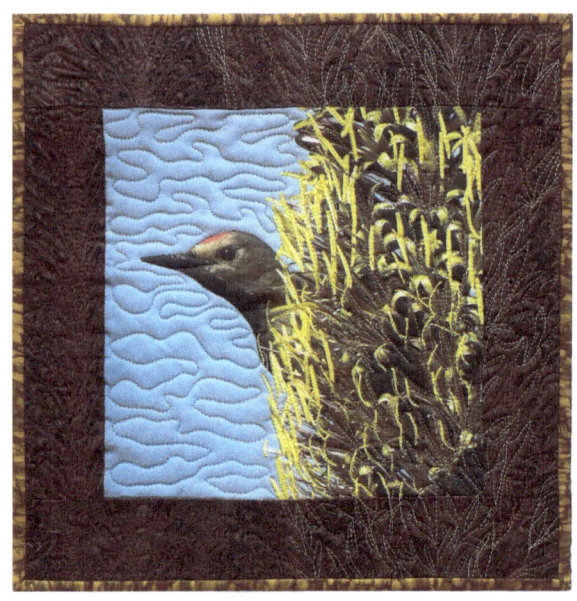

PEEK-A-BOO

POSTCARD QUILTS

The quilts in the size of a large post card are either printed photos or fused appliquéd. They always make nice gifts.

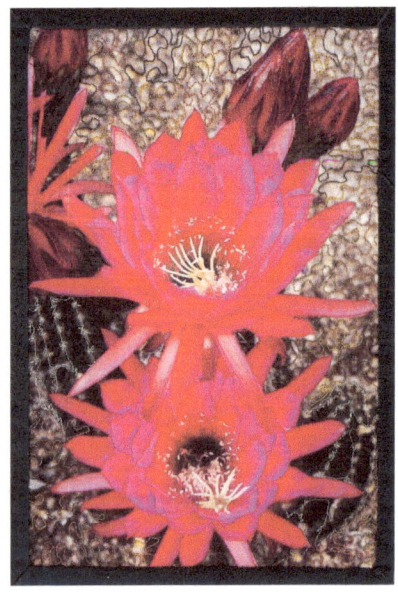

CEREUS BLOSSOMS

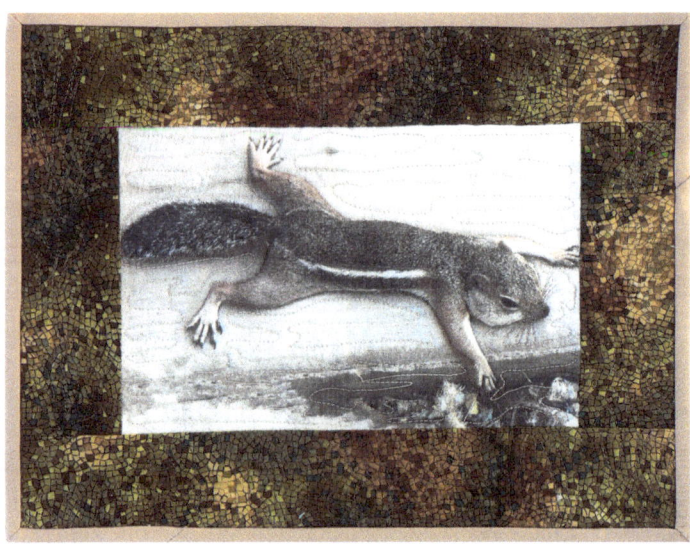

COOL!

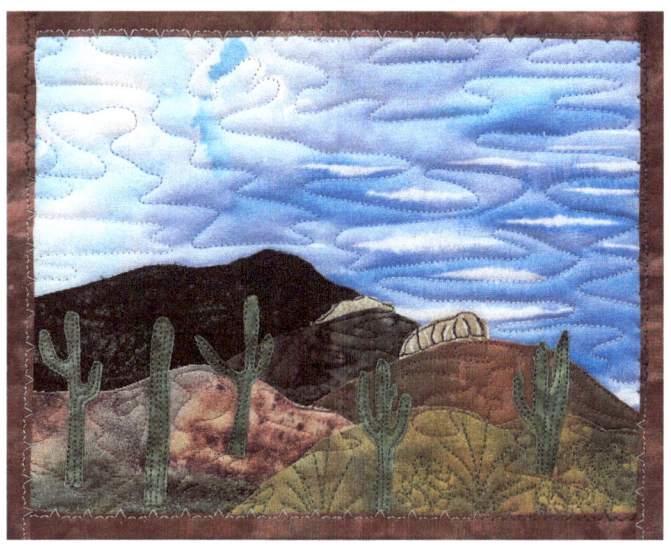

ELEPHANT BUTTE

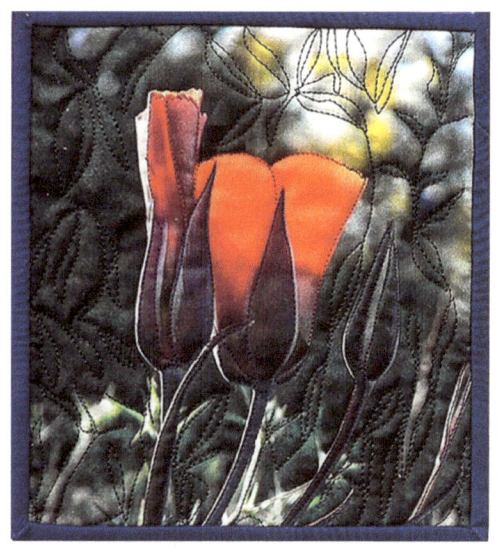

MARIPOSA LILY

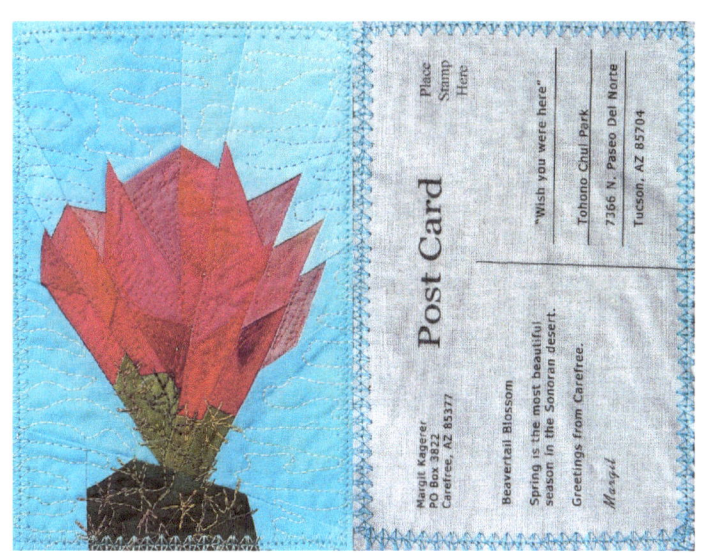

BEAVERTAIL BLOSSOM

This fabric card was sent with mail service to Tucson for an exhibition at the Tohono Chul Park.

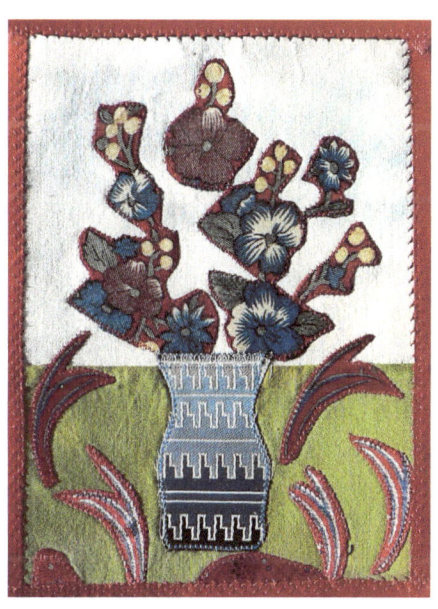

SENDING FLOWERS

NEW MATERIALS

I started using neckties in my quilts in 2001. In the beginning I was not sure how to work with this material that is different from the cotton fabrics I had used until then. It was hard to do the traditional piecing with this stretchy and soft material. I experimented with machine appliqué with the edges turned under, then raw edge appliqué, and fusing. I also utilized that the ties have already a finished edge when they are not totally opened up. Especially the large and small ends are perfect for hand or machine appliqué. With my increasing stash of neckties my experience of working with them grows too.

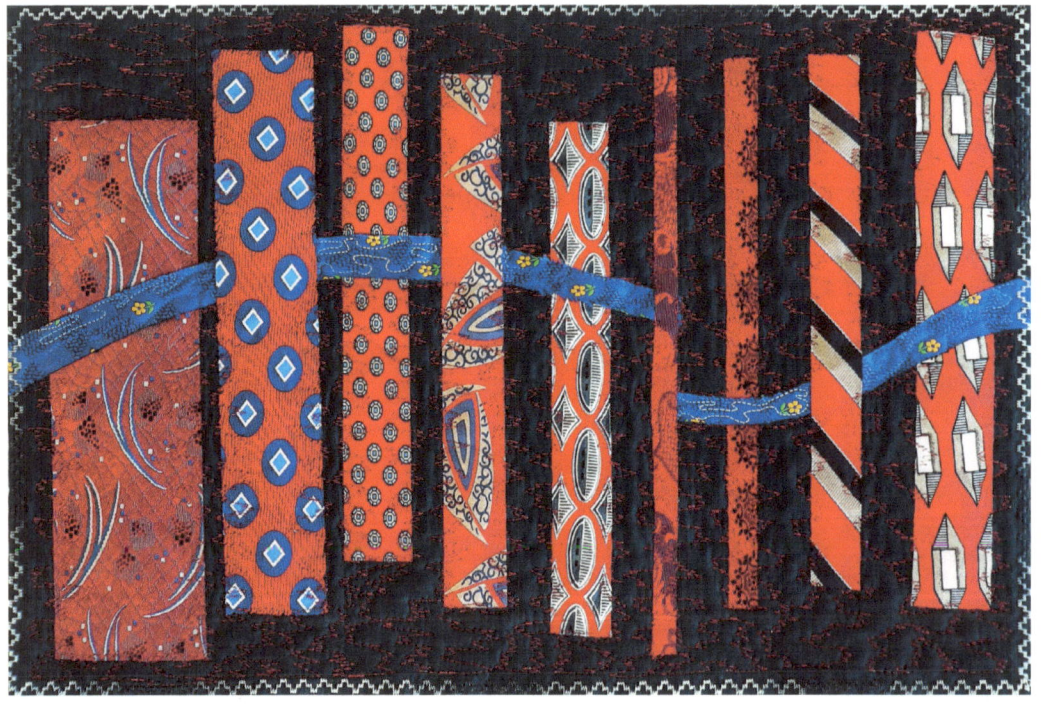

REDS

© Margit Kagerer, 2010, 15" x 10"

This study with red neckties was made for a gift exchange.

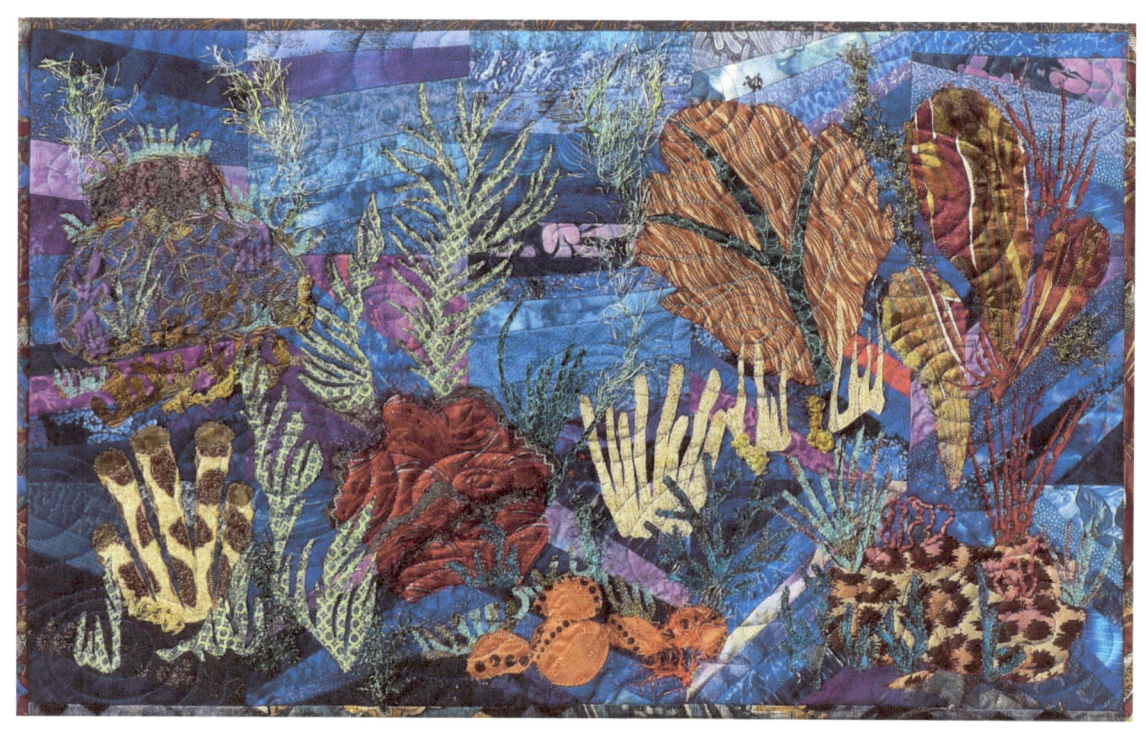

TIE-DAL POOL

© Margit Kagerer, 2009, 31" x 19"

For the background I used many scraps of blue fabrics. I found 'exotic'
ties for all the colorful salt water plants and corals. Fuzzy yarns became
delicate ferns and algae.

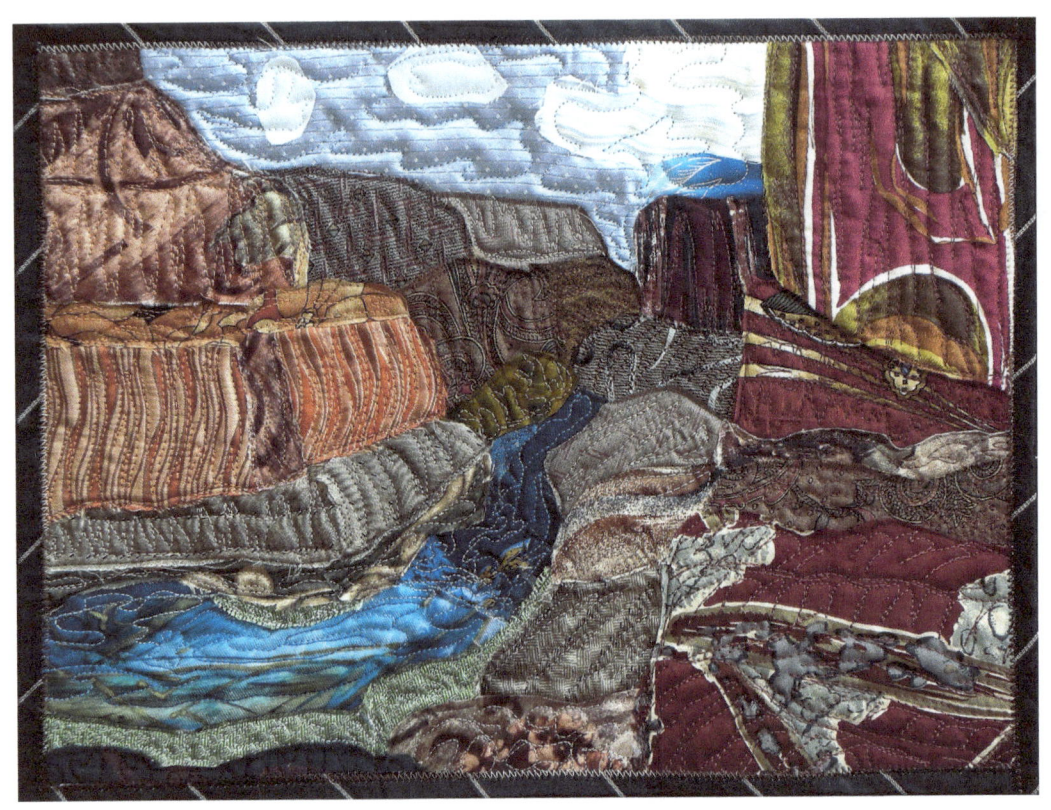

INTO THE CANYON

© Margit Kagerer, 2013, 14" x 10"

When I make my Southwestern landscapes with neckties I leave my comfort zone. Most of my other quilts are pieced with turned under edges. Not the necktie landscapes. The raw edge appliqué technique gives these quilts texture like an expressionistic painting.

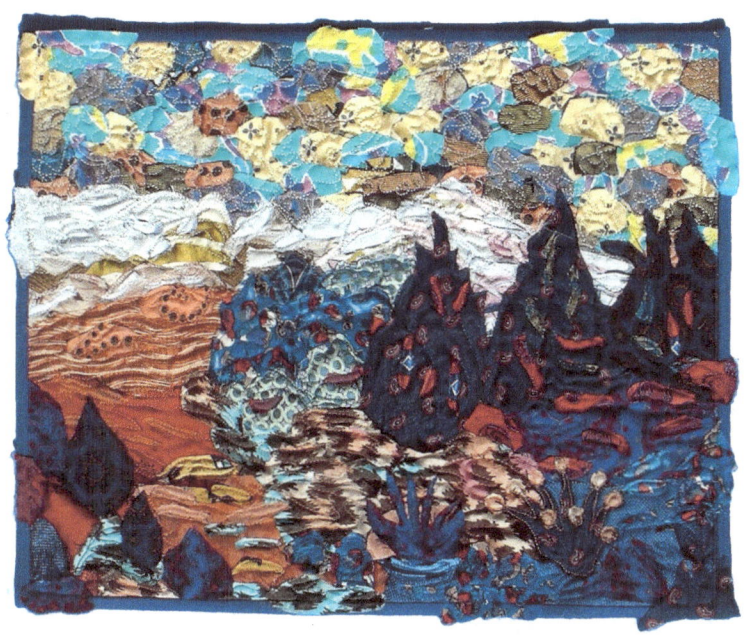

CLAUDIA'S PAINTING

© Margit Kagerer, 2007, 17" x 13"

Claudia Hartley is a wonderful artist. I met her in Arizona and we became friends. She gave me permission to use one of her paintings as a model for a quilt.

Claudia wrote: *"I like to look for shapes in nature to paint. I think of my paintings as similar to a patchwork quilt. Color excites me, and I enhance what is there or even change it completely. But I still keep the patterns of dark and light. When Margit said she wanted to do an actual quilt of my painting, I was thrilled. She made it out of men's neckties and I hang it on the wall next to the painting."*

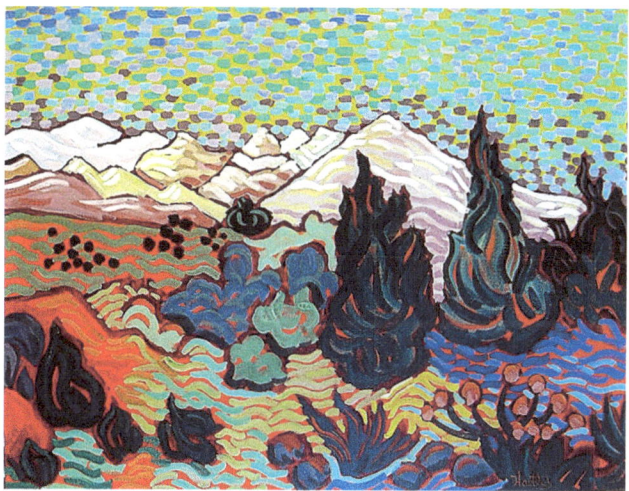

Layers is a series of 15 small quilts where I fused necktie pieces to a foundation and then embellished with decorative stitches. Each piece is approximately 10" x 8".

On the following two pages are **Layer** samples.

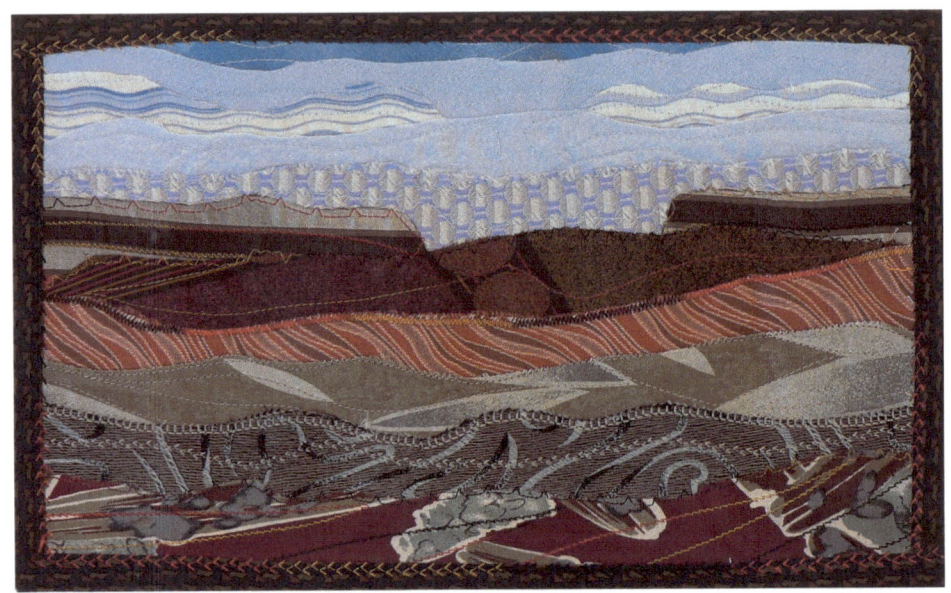

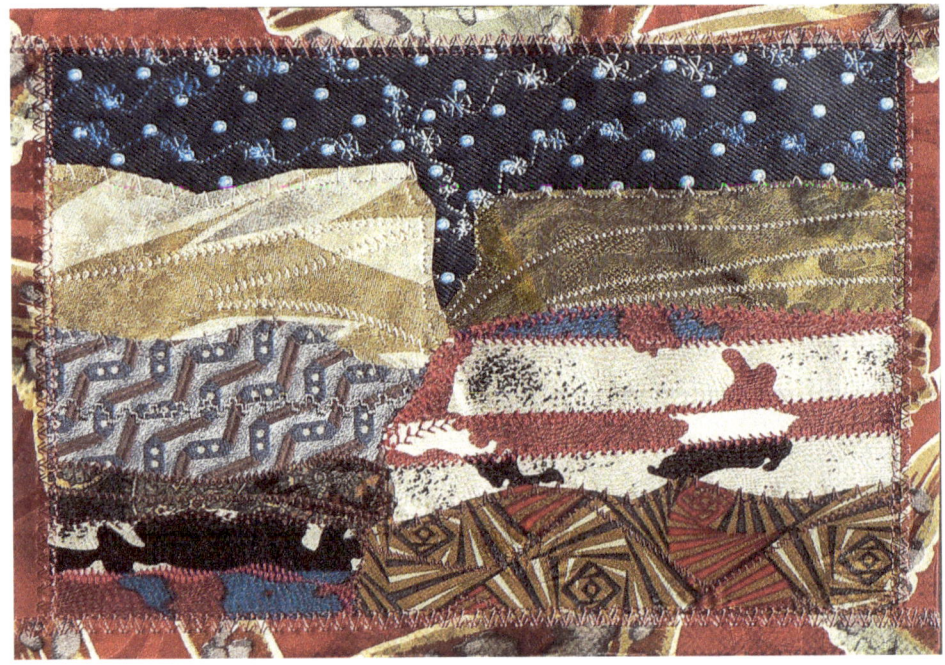

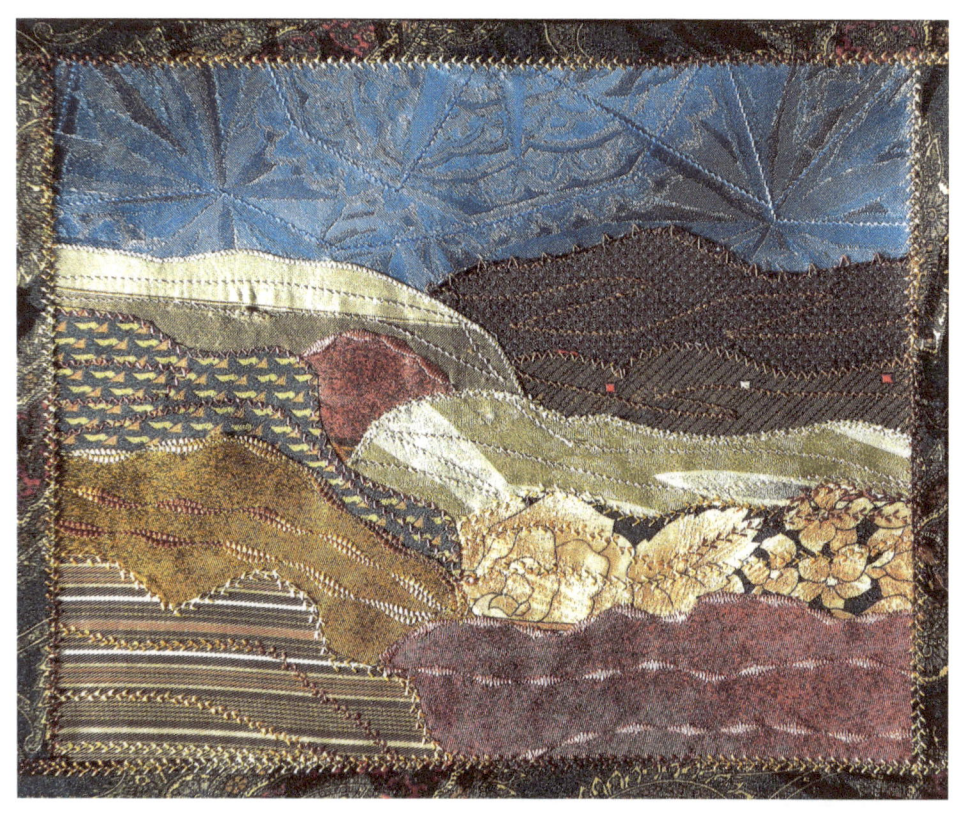

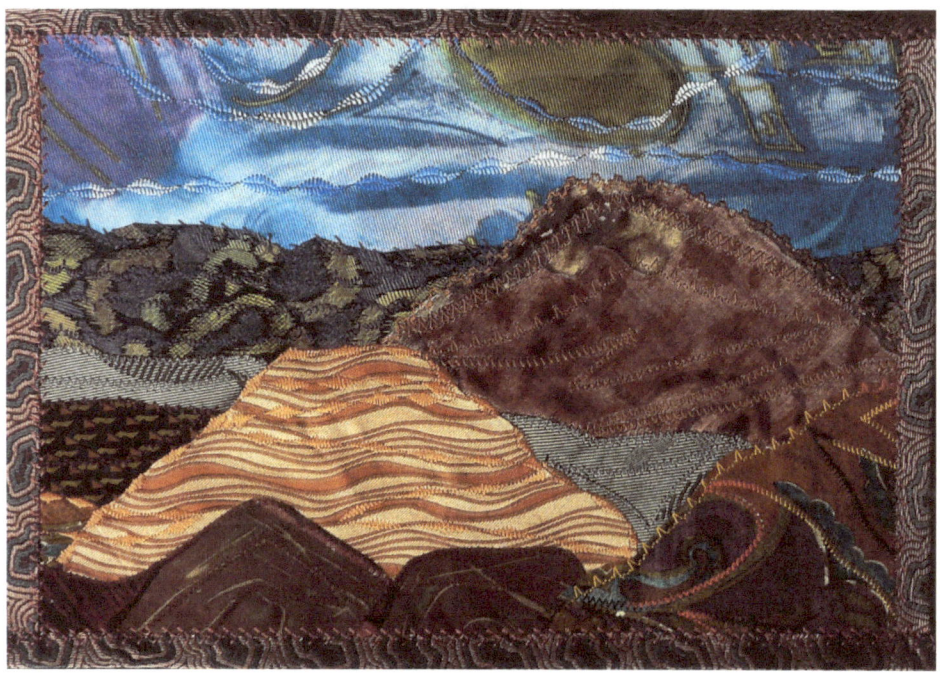

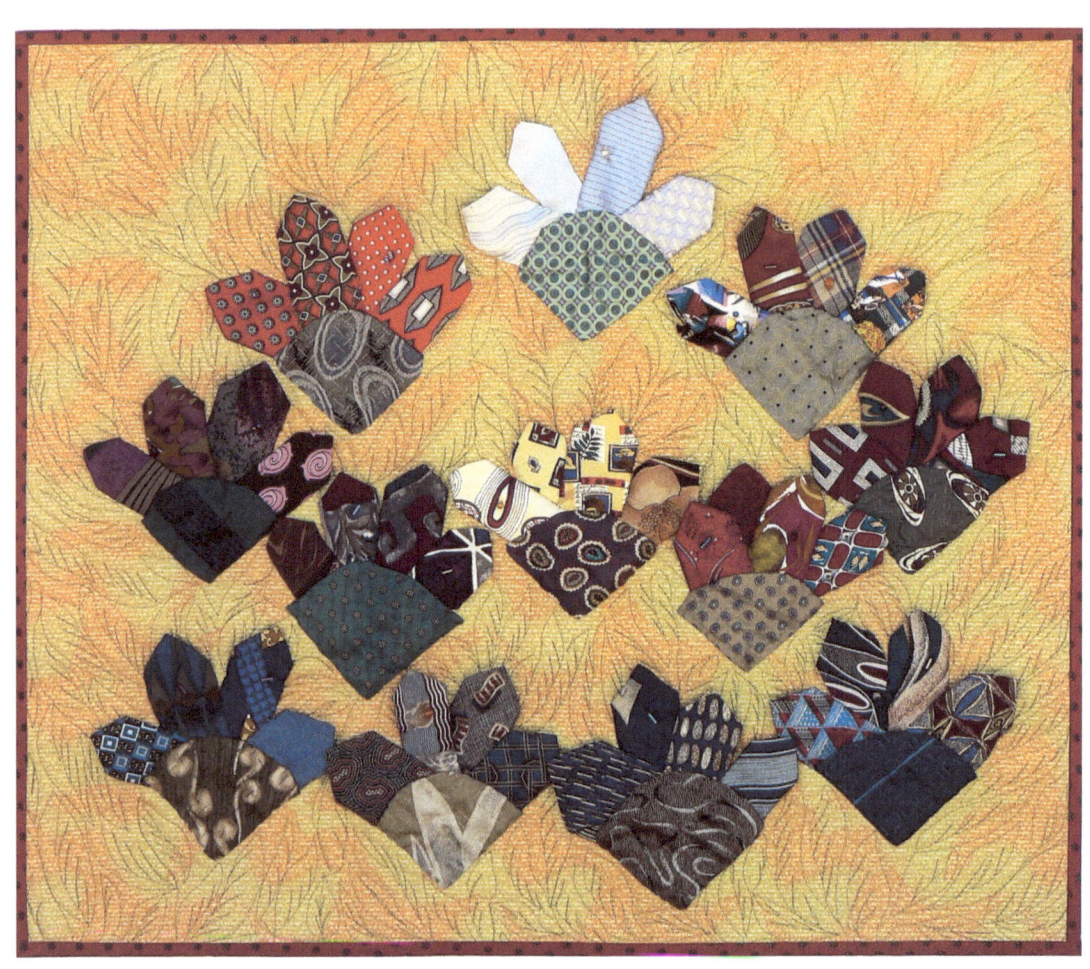

DOES DAD KNOW WHERE HIS TIES ARE?

© Margit Kagerer, 2011, 24" x 20"

First I machine quilted 12 traditional basket blocks surrounded by leaves.
Then I hand appliquéd the small ends of ties in the shape of flower baskets.

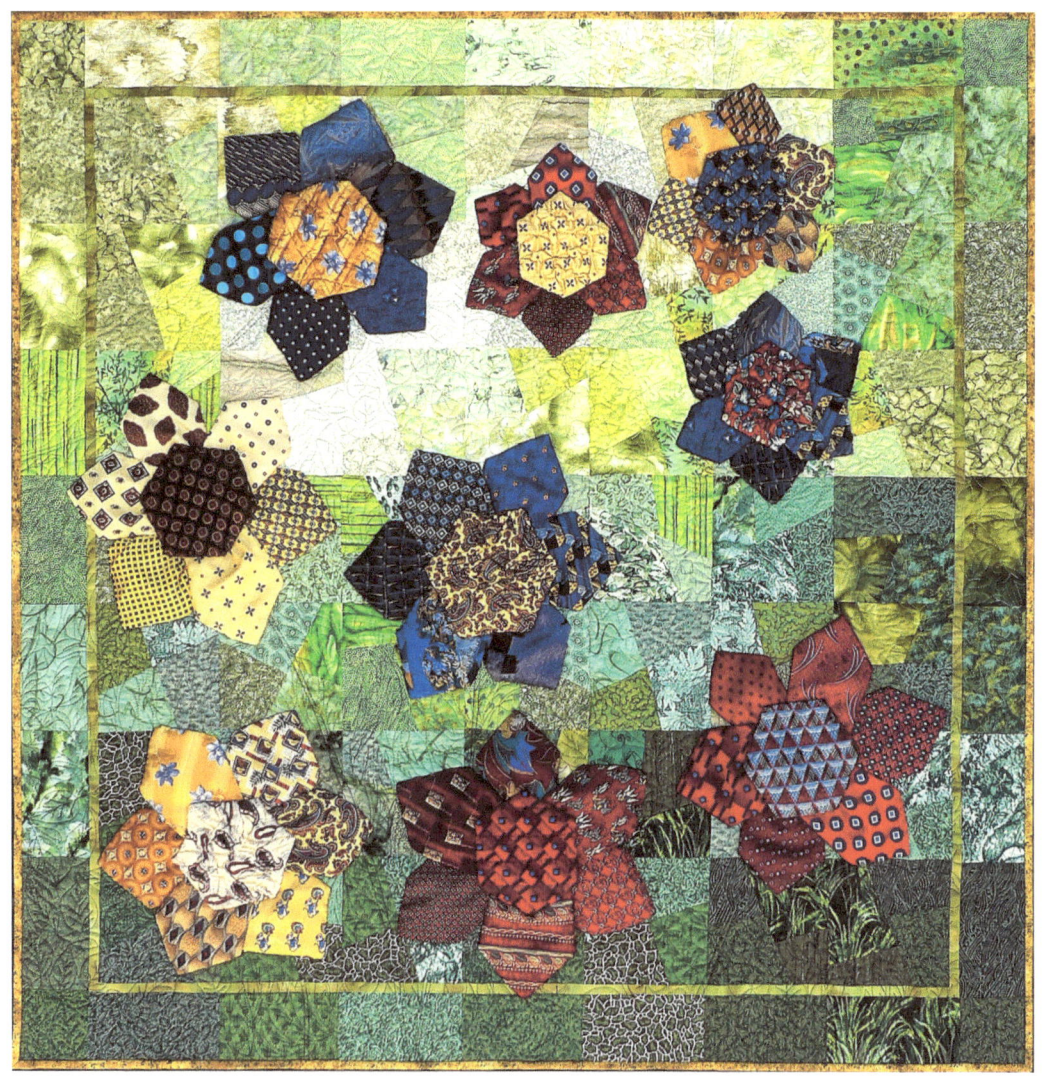

GRANDFATHER'S FLOWER GARDEN

© Margit Kagerer, 2012, 42" x 42"

Grandfather was quite innovative when he designed his garden. He only kept the traditional hexagon shapes of grandmother's flower garden. For the background, he used many scraps of green fabrics. Then he went through his stash of old neckties and revived them for the flowers. He machine quilted different leaves in a free motion way.

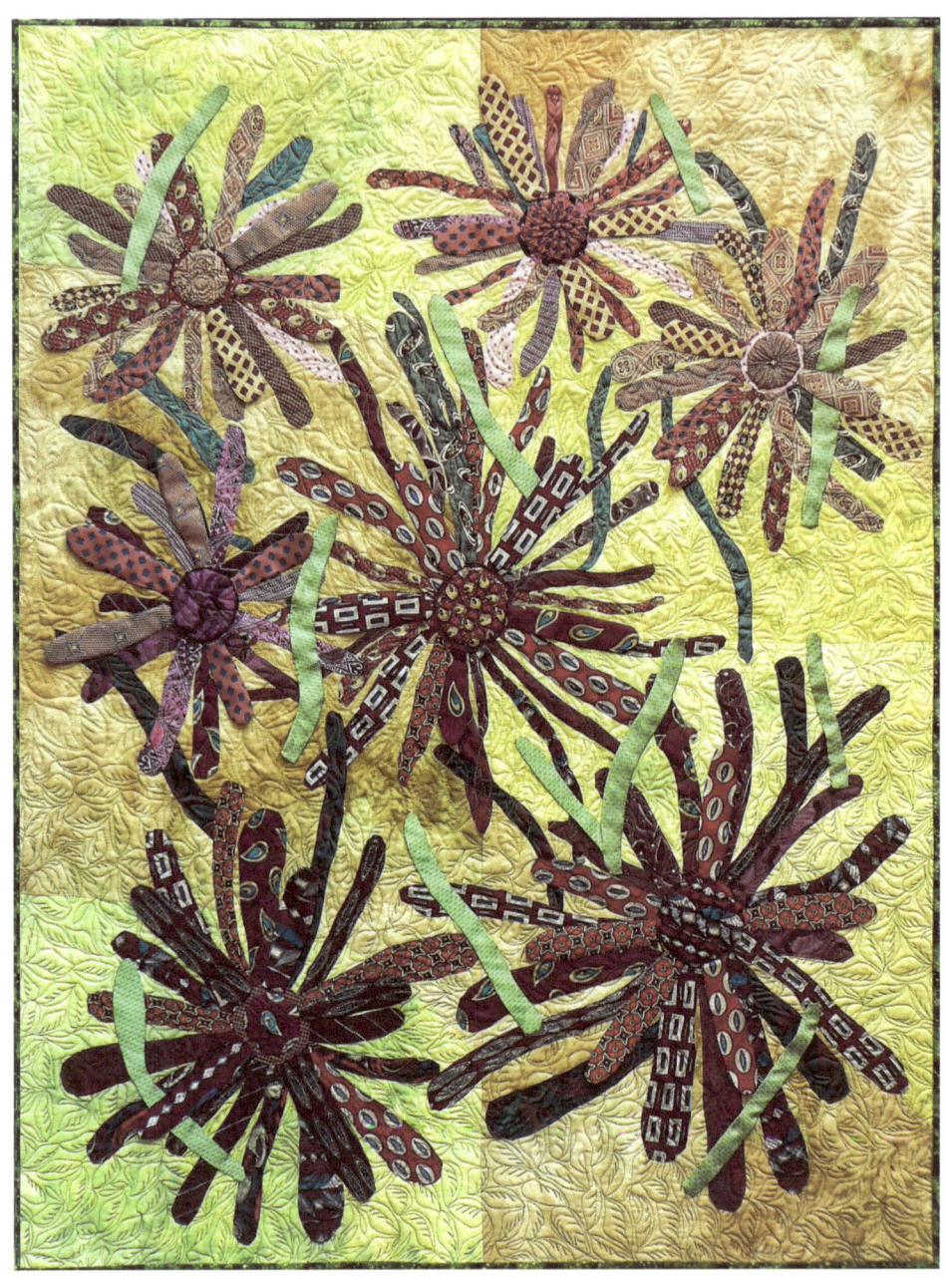

TIE A BOUQUET OF FLOWERS

© Margit Kagerer, 2012, 41" x 53"

In my necktie series I work with the material in many different ways. For this quilt I appliquéd very long pieces of neckties to create the petals of my fantasy flowers. The three-dimensional centers are made with a texturizing product. I used many different shades of reds but it was hard to find a dusty pink necktie.

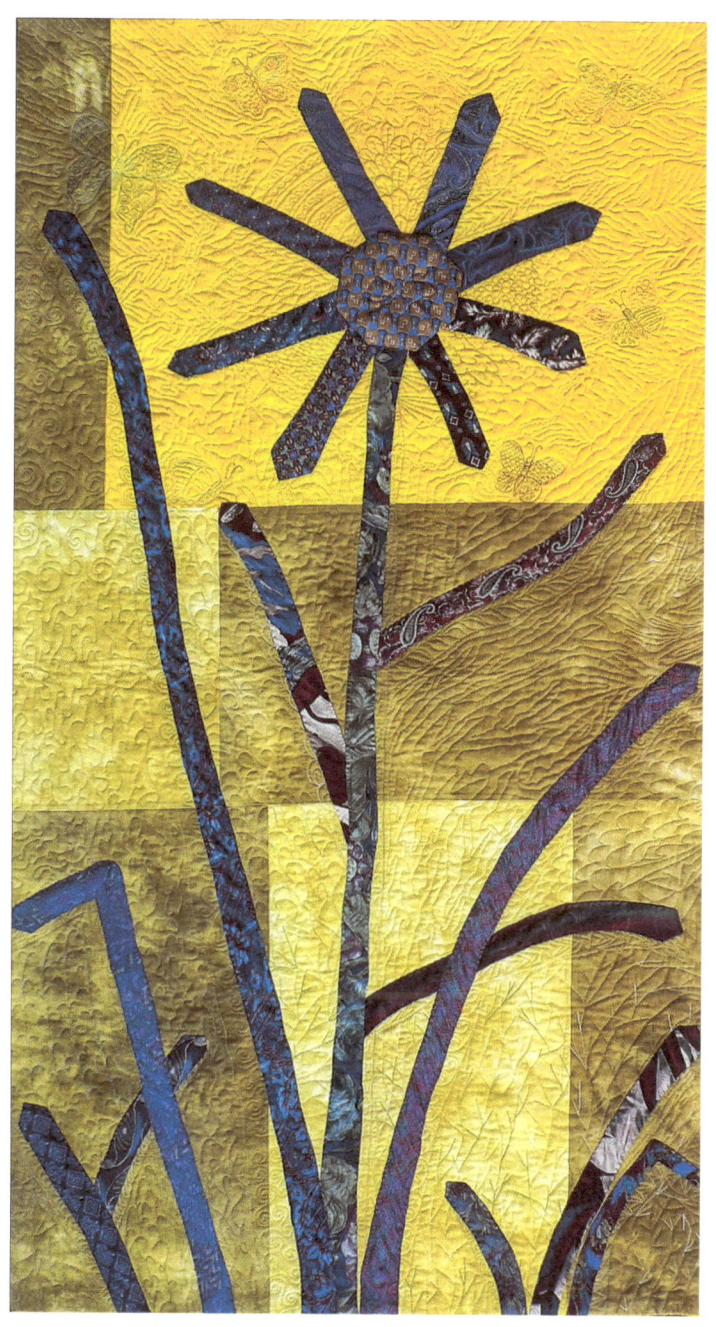

TALL TIE-FLOWER

© Margit Kagerer, 2014, 31" x 60"

For this single flower I picked the most attractive neckties in my stash. I took only the lining out and left the ties as long as possible to show all the detailed patterns in the fabrics. So the flower grew quite tall. To balance the straight structure I quilted curly and cheerful lines that were inspired by zentangles.

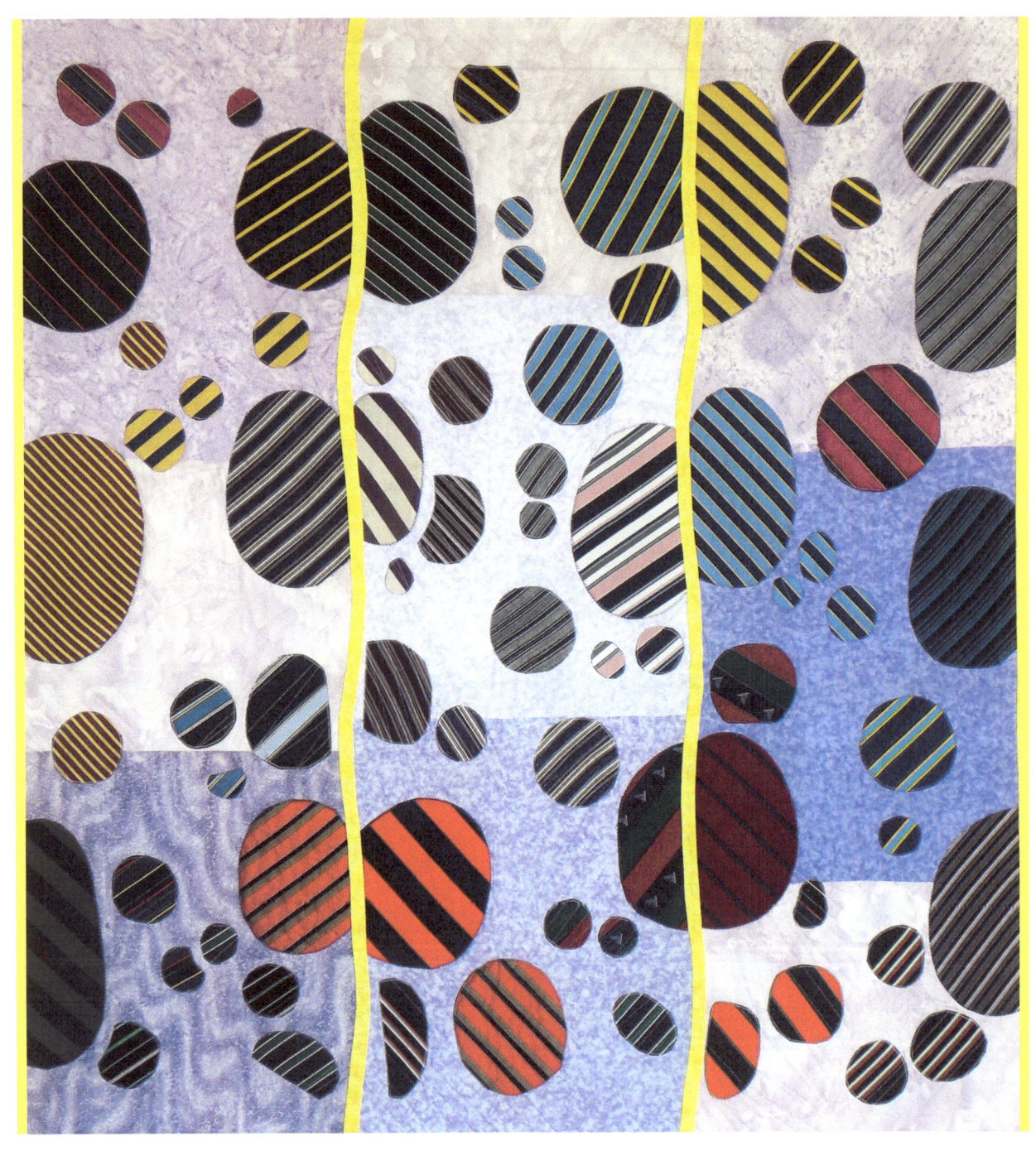

EFFERVESCENCE #1

© Margit Kagerer, 2013, 48" x 51"

13 years ago I got a bag full of neckties. Over the years my stash grew and I tried out many different techniques. In this quilt I raw-edge appliquéd the necktie pieces. The fun part was to find all the striped neckties within my American and European ties. Never before had I realized that the stripes in American neckties slant in the opposite direction of the stripes in British neckties. This became the main design element for my quilt.

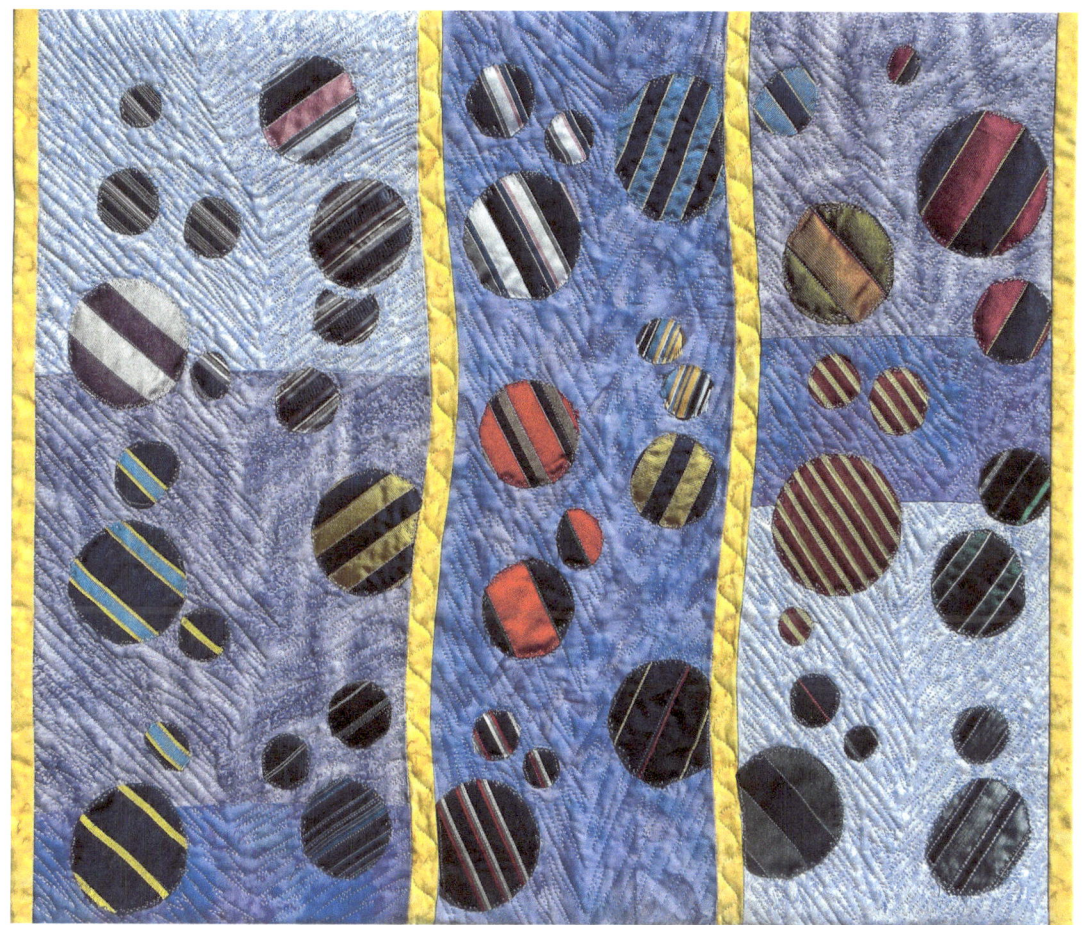

EFFERVESCENCE #2

© Margit Kagerer, 2013, 27" x 21"

2 is the smaller 'sibling' of #1. I still have striped ties for many more quilts.

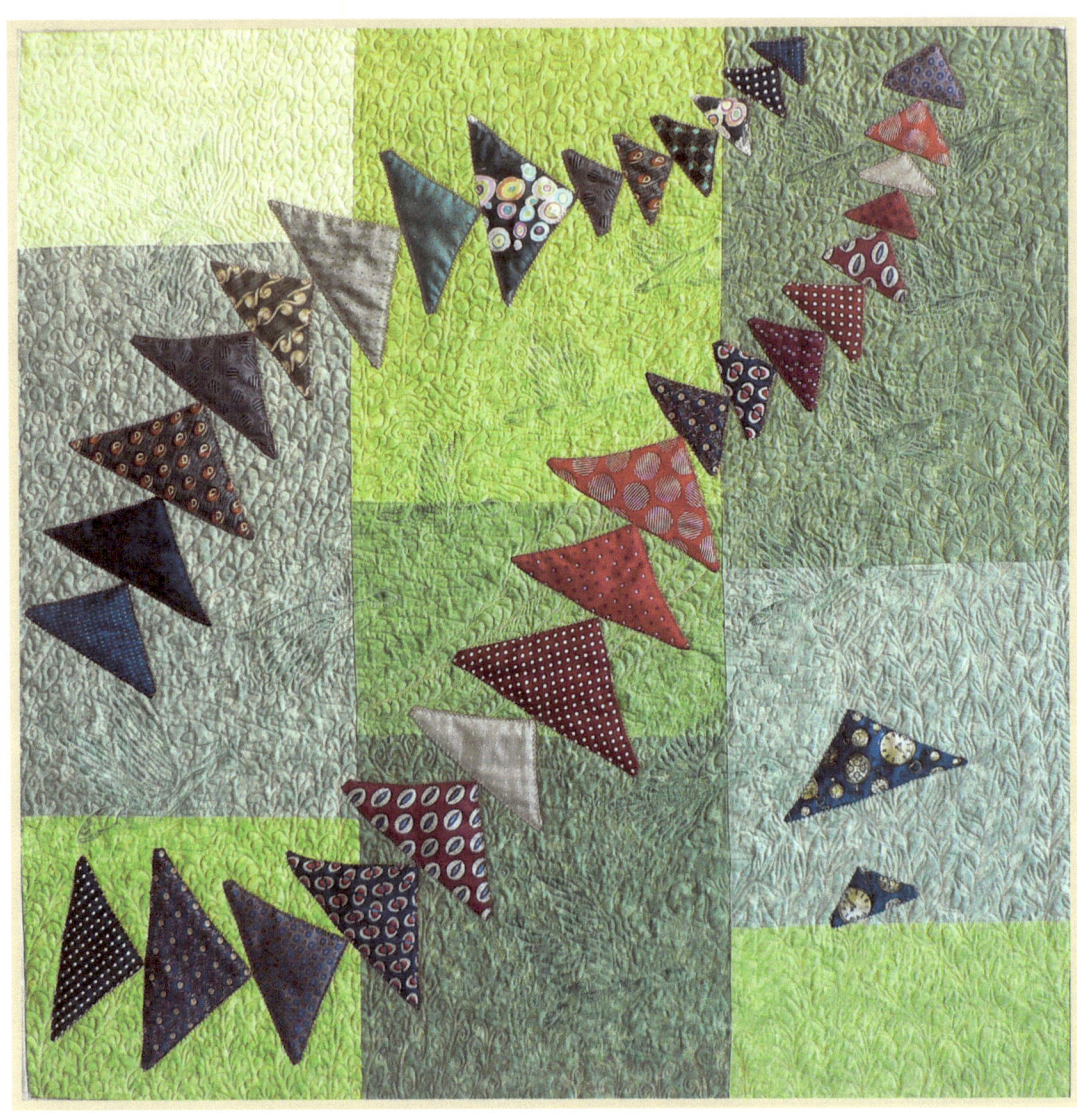

IT'S TIME TO JOIN THE SKEIN

© Margit Kagerer, 2013, 47" x 47"

After all the striped ties in Effervescence #1 and #2 I chose ties with all kinds of dots. As a contrasting shape I picked triangular pieces. The ends of the ties were ideal for the machine appliqué with a decorative stitch. When I investigated the flight of geese I learned that the V-formation is also called a skein. I machine quilted different feather patterns and the images of geese.

OFFICE WARRIORS – NOT ON CASUAL FRIDAYS

© Margit Kagerer, 2014, 39" x 42"

Like the Chinese terra cotta soldiers, my office warriors are lining up for work, ready to enter a tall office building. Since it is not casual Friday, they all have to wear neckties. Their names and thoughts about work are quilted around each person.

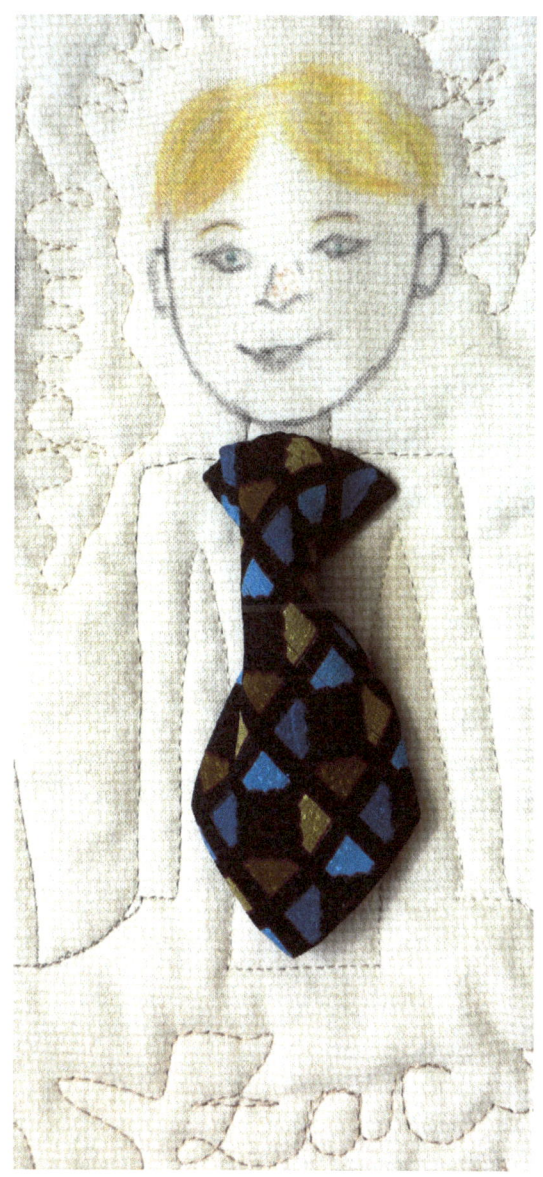

I am ZAC: *Work is fun*

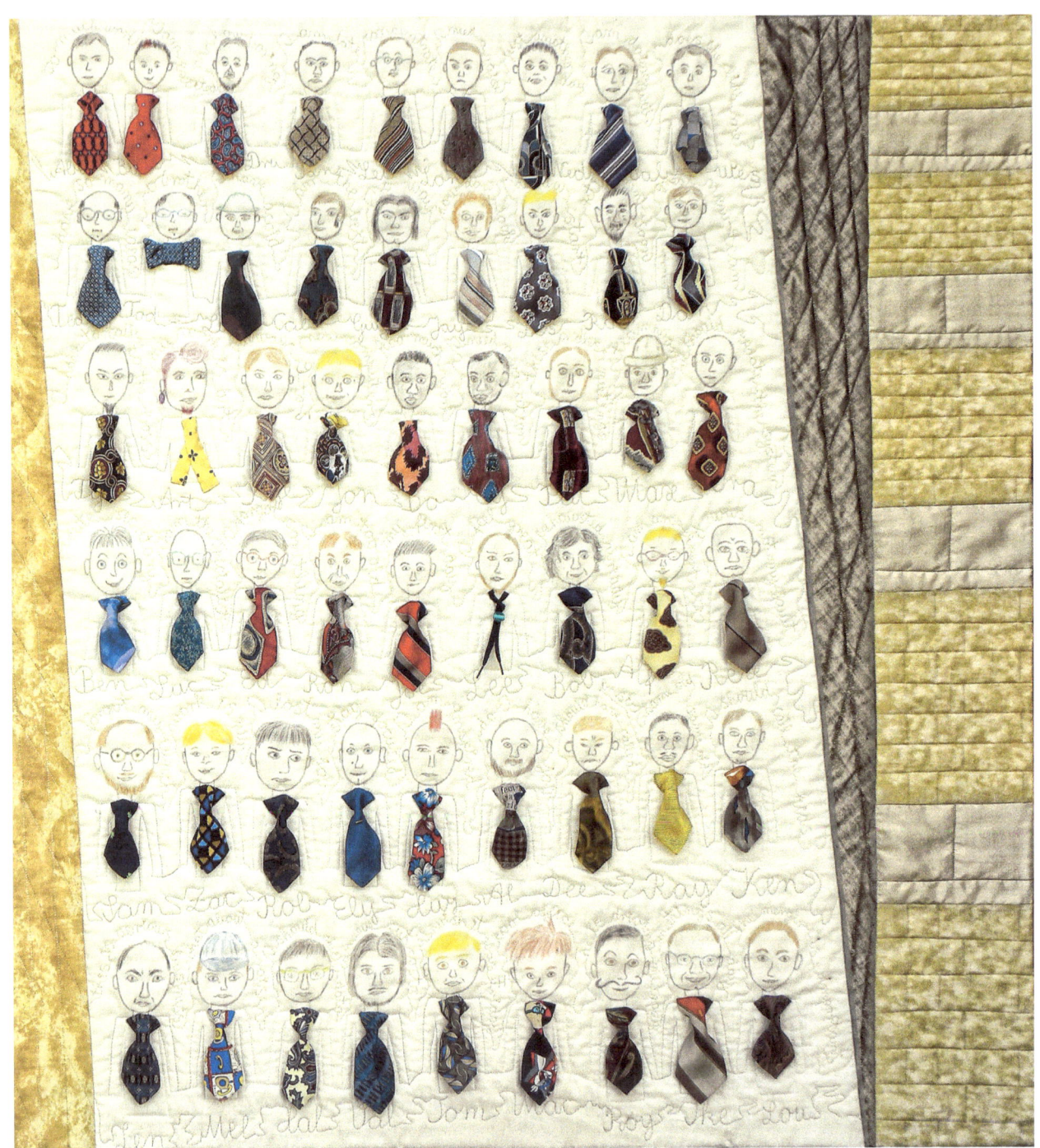

46

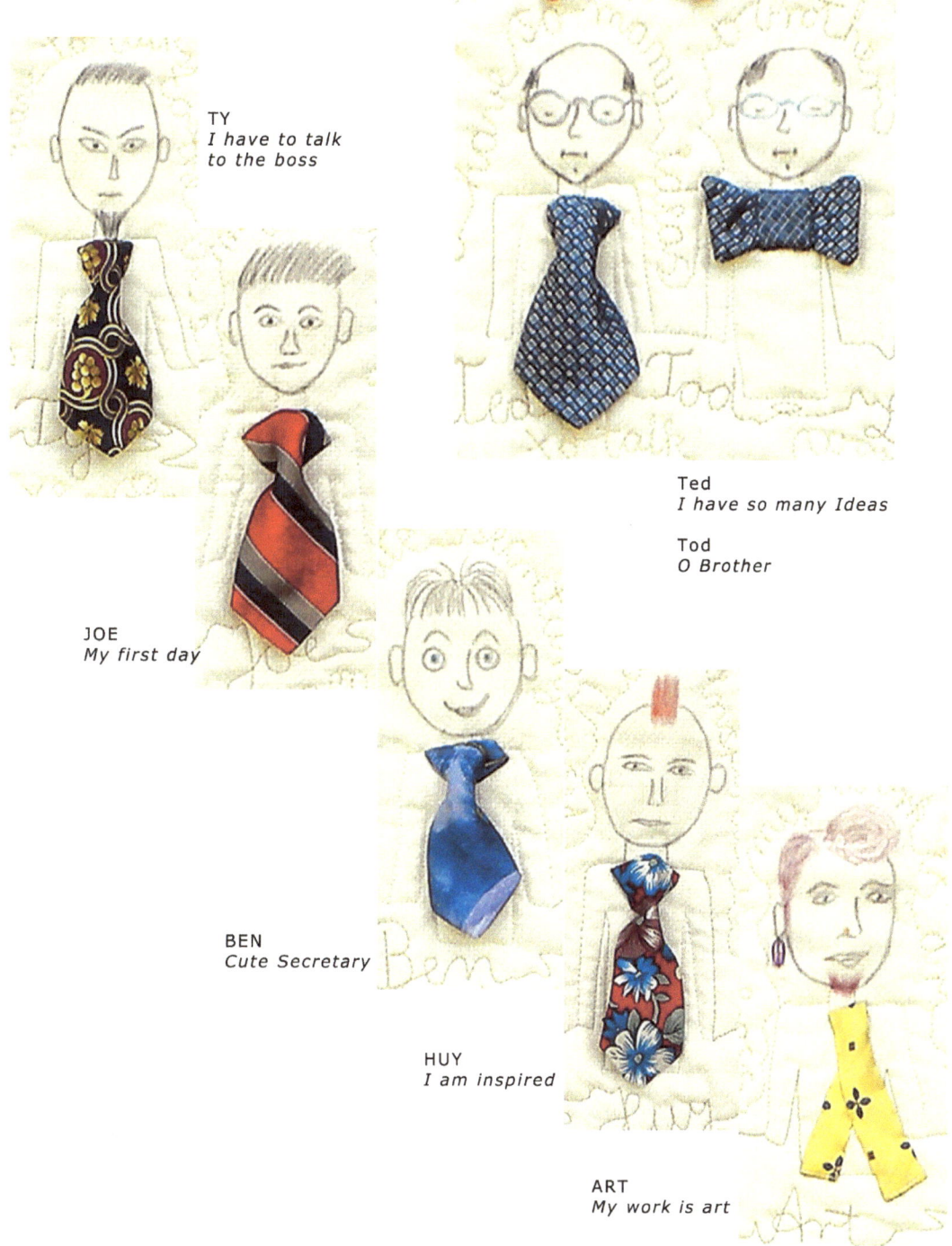

TY
I have to talk to the boss

Ted
I have so many Ideas

Tod
O Brother

JOE
My first day

BEN
Cute Secretary

HUY
I am inspired

ART
My work is art

47

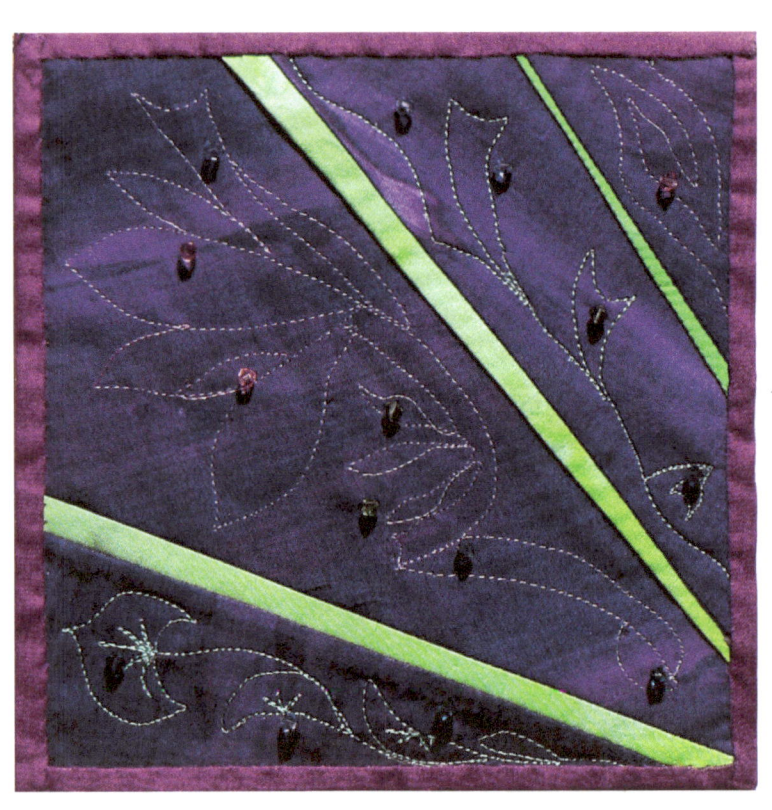

www.ingramcontent.com/pod-product-compliance
Lightning Source LLC
Chambersburg PA
CBHW050815180526
45159CB00004B/1674